Striker Jones

Second Edition

TEACHER'S COMPANION

Elementary Economics for Elementary Detectives

Striker Jones

Second Edition

TEACHER'S COMPANION

Elementary Economics for Elementary Detectives

By Maggie M. Larche

Novel Contents

1. Shark Showdown	1
2. The Missing Key	11
3. Risky Decisions	25
4. Looks Like Love	37
5. Election Day	49
6. Smarts and Crafts	59
7. Auction Action	67
8. The Egg Hunt Hoodwink	79
9. Museums and Mummies, Dinos and Daisies	89
10. The Surprise Story	101

Additional Teacher's Companion Resources

Lesson plans follow each chapter.

At Back:

Glossary of possible vocabulary words divided by chapter.

Alignment to Common Core and National Council on Economic Education standards.

Chapter 1

Shark Showdown

It was late August when Striker Jones and his best friend, Bill Flannagan, were at the beach for one last day of summer fun. With a new school year starting the next day, they decided to commemorate the end of summer the best way they knew how.

"Let's dig a hole," said Striker.

"You're on," said Bill.

They set to work hollowing out a crater in the white sand as the sun beat down on their heads.

"I'm not stopping until we hit water," said Bill, raking a pile of sand with his hands.

"Unless it's for ice cream," said Striker.

"Or girls," added Bill.

Striker laughed. "Deal."

The two boys worked in a comfortable silence, occasionally whistling or telling the odd joke or two. They'd been best friends for years, and digging a hole had become one of their yearly traditions. They each had their own separate part to play. Striker was of medium height, so he would loosen the sand. Meanwhile, Bill, who was very tall, would shovel the sand out of the hole.

They had made it down about two feet, when Striker looked up and noticed another friend at the beach—Zack Marcus. Zack was the same age as Striker and Bill and was scheduled to be in their class during the next year.

Usually, Striker thought Zack was a pretty normal guy, but right then, he was doing something rather peculiar in the water. Zack was standing where the beach pier jutted out into the water. The water was a little rough there, yet he wasn't paying any attention to the waves crashing around his shoulders. "Not the safest spot to be daydreaming," thought Striker, when he noticed that Zack was staring intently at something he held in his hand.

"Look," said Striker to Bill, where he was lying down on the sand to reach deeper into the hole. "Zack is here, and I think he found something."

Bill raised himself up on one elbow. "What's he got?"

"Dunno," said Striker. "But he's coming back to shore. Let's ask him."

Out in the water, Zack was working his way onto shore, fighting the waves that kept breaking and threatening to knock him over. A few minutes later, Zack reached the beach near Striker and Bill. He flopped onto his back, breathing heavily from the trek.

"Hey, Zack," called Bill. "Whatcha got there?"

Zack rolled over so that he could see Striker and Bill. "Oh, hey, guys." He sat up and brushed the sand off his stomach. "Look what I just found in the water!" He held out his open palm, in which lay a brown, pointy rock.

Striker squinted in the sun to see the object better.

"Wow," he said. "Looks like an arrowhead!"

"Yep," said Zack with a grin. "Isn't it awesome?"

"Cool!" said Bill. "Can I see it?"

"Sure," said Zack, handing over the rock. "I bet it's really old. It was probably even made by Indians."

"But how did it end up in the ocean?" asked Bill.

"Well," said Zack, "my dad told me once that lots of the rivers around here run into the ocean. So, maybe this was just washed in from somewhere inland."

"Makes sense," said Striker.

"You know," said Bill, turning the stone over in his hands, "I've always really wanted one of these. Would you be willing to make a trade?"

"A trade?" asked Zack, raising an eyebrow. "For what?"

"Well…" Bill paused, thinking. "How about that Swift Rogers baseball card you've been asking me about for so long?"

Zack sat straight up. "Really?" He seemed surprised that Bill was making such a valuable offer.

"Totally," said Bill. "I love Indian stuff."

"You've got a deal, mister!"

"Cool. I'll bring you the card tomorrow at school."

The two boys shook on it, and Striker and Bill went back to digging their hole.

One hour later, the hole was so big that they could both stand up in it and just barely see over the side.

"I've gotta say," said Bill, inside the hole, "we've dug some awesome holes, but I think this one might be the biggest."

"I know," said Striker, standing next to him. "We finally hit water!" And it was true—there was a little puddle of water at their feet from the ground. "Let's see if we can get it even deeper."

"Ok," said Bill, "but first, I'm going to dunk in the ocean. It is so hot out here!" He climbed out of the hole and brushed the sand off of himself. "Be right back."

Striker squatted down in the hole and began using his hands to loosen the sand.

Just as he was thinking he might need a bucket to finish the job, he heard someone talking nearby. It sounded like Zack.

"Uh oh," Zack was muttering quietly. "Not over there." Suddenly, Zack raised his voice to a yell. "Bill, um, Bill! Don't go over there!"

"Why not?" Striker faintly heard Bill's voice come drifting back from across the water.

"Because… um, because," Zack yelled, "because there's… a shark!"

Striker sat up in surprise.

"What?" Bill called back.

"I said, SHARK!" yelled Zack.

This time Striker sprang into action as did the twenty or so other children who had been swimming nearby. Striker half jumped and half climbed out of his hole while the many swimmers all made a mad dash for shore.

When Striker appeared beside Zack so suddenly, Zack gave an impressive jump of surprise.

"Striker?" he almost shouted. "Where'd you come from?"

"I was in the hole," said Striker. "Where's the shark?" He peered out at the water.

"Oh, the shark?" said Zack. "He was, um, over there by the pier where Bill was. I spotted his fin coming out of the water."

"Wow," said Striker, "it's a good thing you were watching!"

Bill had just emerged from the water at a swift run.

"Geez!" he wheezed out. "That was the fastest I've ever moved in my life!" He leaned over to catch his breath as swimmers dashed by them. "Thanks, Zack! I really appreciate you sounding the alarm!"

"Oh, no problem," said Zack. "Really, it's no big deal."

"No big deal!" said Bill. "You could have just saved someone's life!"

"I still haven't seen the shark though," said Striker. "Where did you say it was?"

"Right by the pier," said Zack, pointing. "We should probably all stay away from there for the day."

"Away from the pier?" asked Bill, laughing. "How about away from the *water*? I know I'm not going back in today!"

"Well, yeah," said Zack. "That, too."

Striker gave Zack a questioning look. "Yeah," he said slowly. "If there was a shark, we'd definitely want to stay away from the pier… If…"

"What do you mean, if?" asked Bill.

Striker looked at Zack, who was now staring guiltily down at his bare feet in the sand. For a moment, Striker did not say anything, until he announced, "Well, I got pretty sandy digging that hole. I think I'll go in to wash off."

"You mean, into the water?" asked Bill incredulously. "You can't do that! It's not safe!"

But Striker had already dived in.

Was it safe?

Solution

When Zack repeatedly insisted that everyone should definitely stay away from the pier, Striker remembered something else about that area. That was where Zack had been when he'd found the arrowhead.

Striker knew that when someone is trading something, he's in a much better position if whatever he's trading is hard to get. Luckily for Zack, arrowheads are very hard to come by, so he was able to make a pretty good trade—the arrowhead for the baseball card. But, when Zack saw Bill getting close to the pier, he panicked. What if his arrowhead wasn't the only one? What if Bill found one too? Then, he wouldn't have been able to trade for the baseball card.

So, Zack panicked and yelled the first thing that came to his mind—shark.

When Striker jumped into the water, Bill had been only seconds from going in after him to save him. But just as Bill was about to take off, Zack stopped him and told the truth. He had only pretended to see a shark.

Zack obviously felt very bad about causing so many people to run scared from the water. So though he offered repeatedly to cancel the trade, Bill decided to keep the deal they had made. The next day, they switched, the baseball card for the arrowhead, and each was happier for it. But after that exchange, Bill didn't propose any more trades with Zack. Just in case.

Striker Jones, "Shark Showdown"

Lesson Plan

Objective: Students will be able to explain and apply the economic concepts of bartering, scarcity, and the mutual benefits of trade.

Procedure

1. Read the chapter "Shark Showdown" up until the Solution, either as a class or separately.

2. In pairs or small groups, have students discuss what they believe is the solution to the mystery.

3. Read the Solution as a class.

4. As a class, define the words *barter* (to trade), *scarcity* (having limited amounts of something), and *benefit* (something that is good).

5. Check for understanding with the following questions:

    - Why did Zack not want Bill to find his own arrowhead? (Because then Bill wouldn't have needed to trade with Zack anymore.)

    - How were both Bill and Zack made better off by completing the trade? (They each ended up with something that they valued more highly than what they'd traded away. Zack would rather have the baseball card; Bill would rather have the arrowhead.)

6. Discuss the concept of barter and scarcity. Key points include the following:

    - All resources are scarce. Whether it means that you only have so much time before you go to bed, or whether the United States is made up of only so much land, we don't have unlimited amounts of anything!

    - With scarce resources, we can barter, or trade, to get the best combination of resources possible. For instance, you can trade goods, like comic books or toys. You could also trade other things that aren't so easy to see and touch, like an extra half hour of playing outside in exchange for doing the dishes.

    - Barter, or trade, is amazing, because it always leaves both sides better off. After all, if a trade didn't make you better off, why would you do it in the first place? This applies whether you're trading between friends or between countries! We call this the mutual benefits of trade.

7. Class Activity: Divide three different kinds of candy among all students. Each student should only have one kind of candy. Then, allow the students to trade with one another for five minutes. At the end of the trading period, ask students to vote on whether they're happier or less happy with where they ended up compared to where they started. Discuss why as a class. Then eat the candy!

Assignment

In the story, Bill makes the trade with Zack even though Zack mislead him about the shark. In the future, though, Bill decides not to trade any more with Zack. In a paragraph, describe why you think that Bill makes this decision. Would you have made the same decision? What does this tell you about how you should behave when you trade with someone?

"Shark Showdown" Lesson

Chapter 2

The Missing Key

Striker shuffled into the classroom with the rest of his classmates after music class. He was feeling cranky, not because he was back in school after a great summer, but because music class had taken a turn for the worst. To his horror, Striker had been the unlucky boy to get picked for a solo that morning.

"During the first week of the year, too!" he thought. "Not a good start."

Now, Striker was good at many things. He was a decent soccer player, was excellent at cards, and could wiggle his ears. But he was no singer.

Of course, he had launched into the solo anyways—Striker was never one to disobey a teacher, especially not Ms. Harper, the music teacher, who was young and pretty—but it had only been with the greatest embarrassment. He cringed as he reached his desk, remembering one particularly bad high note he'd just barely managed to squeak out.

The boy sitting next to Striker, Ralph Johnson, noticed his expression and laughed. Striker had known Ralph for years. They'd been neighbors, and enemies, since they were five years old. Striker had been very disappointed to discover that Ralph was not only in his class this year, but was assigned to sit next to him.

"Hey, that was some show, Striker!" laughed Ralph, pushing up his glasses. "But I don't think I'd sign on with a band just yet. Unless it's a bunch of yodelers!"

Striker rolled his eyes but stayed silent. He would have liked to think of something clever to say back, but secretly he agreed with Ralph. So, he turned his back to him and tried to distract himself from Ralph's snickering with a conversation his teacher, Ms. Peters, was having with her teacher's aide, Laura.

"I'm going to run get a soda," Laura was saying. "Do you want me to grab you one too? It's almost lunchtime."

"Thanks," said Ms. Peters, adjusting her ponytail. "That would be great. Hold on and let me give you the fifty cents."

Ms. Peters gave some change to Laura and requested a Dr. Pepper.

"No problem," said Laura, walking to the teacher's desk and picking up a key. After turning from the desk, she almost bumped into two visitors to the classroom. One was a girl with two long red braids down her back whom Striker had never seen before. Behind her stood the principal.

"Ah," thought Striker. "Must be a new student. Well, at least it will take the attention off of me."

Sure enough, moments later, Ms. Peters walked the new girl to the front of the room and signaled for silence. Striker was surprised to see that the girl didn't look uncomfortable at all. He would have been shy in her position.

"Class," said Ms. Peters, "I'd like you all to meet our new student, Amy Beckham. Can we give her a warm greeting?"

"Hi, Amy," the class dutifully repeated.

"Hi," replied Amy looking out at the room with her arms crossed.

Ms. Peters showed Amy to her seat, while the principal waved and walked out the door. Then Ms. Peters began their science lesson of the day. They were learning about different kinds of rocks, and she had examples to show them of each kind.

During the lesson, Laura returned, setting the sodas and the key down on Ms. Peter's desk.

Fifteen minutes later, Ms. Peters announced that she had hidden several different kinds of rocks around the room while the students were at music class.

"There are enough rocks for each student to find one," she said. "So, once you've found one, you're to go back to your seat and try to identify what kind of rock you've got. Everyone understand?" The class nodded. Striker felt the students around him tensing for action, and he hid a laugh as he watched his friend Bill tighten his shoelaces.

"Ok, then," said Ms. Peters. "Try not to get too wild," she added, looking pointedly at Ralph. "Ready? Go!

All the students jumped up, but Striker dropped to the ground and started searching under the desks around him. Just when Striker's hand had closed over a grey stone he'd discovered under Bill's backpack, he heard Ralph shout, "I found one," from the direction of Ms. Peters's desk. He looked up to see Ralph crawling out from under the teacher's desk, holding a white, shiny rock.

Striker and Ralph both returned to their seats to examine their rocks. Several people were still looking, including the new girl Amy, but one by one, everyone returned to their seats and tried to classify their rocks. Striker had just decided that his rock must be sedimentary, when Ms. Peters announced that time was up.

"It's lunchtime," she said. "I hope you've figured your rock out, because we're going to discuss them when we get back."

The students all jumped out of their chairs and lined up at the door.

"Let's go," said Ms. Peters, leading the students into the hall.

Nobody noticed that something was missing from the teacher's desk.

In the cafeteria, all the students scrambled for good seats. Striker hurried to get a seat beside Bill and found himself across the table from Sheila Meyers, a short girl with blue eyes. Striker thought Sheila was easily the prettiest girl in school, though of course he never would tell anyone else that.

"This is more like it," he thought. "Maybe my day's going to get better." He opened his lunchbox. It contained one non-fat granola bar and a bologna sandwich.

"Or maybe not," he thought with a sigh.

"Hey," said Sheila, breaking into his thoughts. "You can sit with us if you like."

Striker looked up confusedly, fighting the waves of nervousness he got whenever Sheila said anything to anybody. Who was she talking to? He turned in his seat and saw the new girl Amy standing behind him.

"Thanks," she said to Sheila, sliding into the open seat next to Striker. "I never know where to sit on the first day."

"You never know? Why, do you switch schools a lot?" asked Bill, leaning around Striker.

"We usually move about once or twice a year," she said. "My dad transfers a lot for work."

"Wow," said Sheila, "that is a lot."

Striker thought, "That explains why she wasn't nervous this morning."

"It's not a big deal," said Amy to Sheila. "Besides, we're actually supposed to stay here a while. So I guess you'll all have to get used to me."

They all laughed.

Bill pulled out his lunch consisting of a peanut butter and jelly sandwich, an apple, and baggie of saltine crackers.

"Crackers?" he said. "I think my mom forgot to buy food. This lunch is kind of scraping the bottom of the barrel."

"It's better than mine," said Striker. "Hey, I dare you to eat all those saltines at once."

"No way!" said Bill. "I'd never make it without a drink, and," Bill peered into his bag, "it looks like my mom didn't pack one. She definitely forgot to go grocery shopping."

"Why don't you buy one from the drink machine?" asked Amy. "I thought I saw one in the hallway."

"I wish I could," said Bill. "A soda sounds good. But I don't have enough money with me. The machine costs 75 cents, and I've only got 60."

Amy put down the sandwich she'd been about to take a bite of. "You've got 60 cents?" she asked.

Bill nodded.

"I tell you what," said Amy. "You give me your 60 cents, and I'll get you a soda."

"But it's not enough!" said Bill.

"Don't worry about that," said Amy. "Consider it a gift from the newbie."

"Well, ok," said Bill, doubtfully, "but I want to pay you back tomorrow."

"Sure," shrugged Amy. She held her hand out for Bill's money, which he gave her, and then headed out the door of the cafeteria.

"Wow," said Sheila. "That was really nice of her."

"I guess," said Striker thoughtfully.

Amy came back a few minutes later holding a can of soda. She passed it on to Bill.

"Thanks!" he said.

Amy just smiled.

"And now," said Bill to Striker, "I believe you dared me to eat all these saltines…"

After lunch, the students were seated back in the classroom. Most were rolling their rocks back and forth across their desks, until Ms. Peters stepped to the front of the class.

"I'm glad to see you're all so excited to get back to work," she said with a smile, "but first, we've got some business to take care of. It seems that during the rock search, a few things got knocked off my desk. I've found most of them on the floor, but one thing is still missing—the key to the teacher's lounge. Let's all take a minute to look around the room please. I know it must be in here somewhere, and it's important that we find it."

As the students pushed back their chairs to join in the search, Bill walked over to Striker.

"You know what, Striker? I don't think this was an accident. I bet it was Ralph who took it," whispered Bill. "It sounds just like the kind of thing he'd do. He's always making trouble. Plus, he was looking for rocks right around the teacher's desk."

"But other people walked by it, too," whispered Striker back. "And besides, why would Ralph want the key to the teacher's lounge?"

"Striker, that's where they keep all the stuff they take away from students! Probably half of the stuff in that pile is from Ralph—he gets something confiscated every day!"

Striker considered the idea silently. He was thinking that maybe Bill had a point, when he suddenly had an idea of his own.

"I'm telling you," Bill was saying, "It was Ralph."

"No," said Striker quietly. "Believe it or not, it wasn't Ralph."

Bill looked surprised.

"And another thing," continued Striker, "You probably don't have to pay Amy back tomorrow." He left Bill with his mouth hanging open, and walked off to find Amy.

Why wouldn't Bill pay Amy back?

Solution

From the beginning, Striker wondered why Amy was willing to buy Bill a soda. They cost 75 cents for students, and Bill only had 60. So that meant that Amy was willing to pay the extra 15 cents to get him a drink. Striker didn't know if Amy was just being extra nice, or if something else was going on.

But once Striker found out the key to the teacher's lounge was missing, he remembered an important conversation he'd overheard that morning. Laura, the teacher's aide, told Ms. Peters that 50 cents was enough to buy a soda, which is less than the 75 cents it takes for students to buy a soda! That told Striker that there was some way for teachers to buy cheaper sodas. And where was the one place that teachers could go and students couldn't? The teacher's lounge.

Striker realized that if Amy had stolen the key, she would have been able to take Bill's 60 cents, buy him a soda for 50 cents, and keep 10 cents for herself in profit!

Striker found Amy searching by the bookshelves. He whispered only one sentence, "turn in the key," causing Amy to give a jump of surprise. Striker walked away immediately, and Amy slowly pulled the teacher's lounge key out of her pocket, still looking after Striker in amazement. Finally, she lifted up the key and called, "Ms. Peters, I found it."

After school that day, Amy caught up to Striker as he was leaving the playground.

"Listen, Striker" she said, looking uncertain. "Thanks for not telling on me. But why didn't you?"

Striker looked at her. "I figured it was your first day in a new school, and maybe you'd rather start out without getting in trouble." He shrugged. "Besides, there's nothing wrong with making money. You just have to be honest while you do it."

"Thanks," said Amy. She paused, and then said, "Is there anything I can do to make it up to you?"

"Don't worry about it," said Striker, and began to walk away.

"Wait!" she called after him. "I, uh… I can sing!"

Striker stopped and turned around suspiciously. Was she going to make fun of him?

"I mean, uh," she stammered, "I heard today that you had some trouble in music this morning." She hurried on, "Not to make you feel bad or anything. But I can sing, so if you ever want any help there, you can ask me."

Striker didn't say anything.

"Well, think about it," said Amy. "I'll see you around."

Striker watched her walk off as he thought about her offer. He wasn't especially interested in taking singing lessons, and he could only imagine how Ralph would tease him if he found out.

On the other hand, he vividly remembered a few of the awful sounds that had come out of his mouth that morning. He even thought he'd heard a dog start howling somewhere outside during his solo, or maybe it was just his own voice echoing back to him.

Striker turned to walk home. "Maybe," he thought to himself, "music lessons might not be a bad idea after all."

Striker Jones, "The Missing Key"

Lesson Plan

Objective: Students will be able to explain and apply the economic concepts of profits, loss, and incentives.

Procedure

1. Read the chapter "The Missing Key" up until the Solution, either as a class or separately.

2. In pairs or small groups, have students discuss what they believe is the solution to the mystery.

3. Read the Solution as a class.

4. As a class, define the words *incentive* (a factor that motivates behavior), *profit* (revenue minus costs, or money coming in less money going out), and *loss* (losing money, the opposite of profit).

5. Check for understanding with the following questions:

    - In the story, Amy makes a profit by buying Bill a soda. How is she able to do this? (The sodas in the teachers lounge only cost 50 cents. So, when Bill gives her 60 cents, she has enough to buy the soda and save some for herself.)

    - How much is her profit? (10 cents)

    - Amy stole the key to the teacher's lounge, which was wrong. However, if she'd been able to get Bill a cheaper soda without stealing the key, would it have been wrong for her to help him? Discuss.

6. Discuss the concepts of incentives and profit. Key points include the following:

    - Incentives are any factors that motivate someone's behavior. Sometimes money is an incentive, but people can be motivated by many non-monetary factors as well, such as wanting to help a friend or a desire to watch a favorite TV show.

    - Profit is a common incentive, particularly for people operating businesses. By working to make a profit, business owners also do good for others by providing goods and services to their customers. If they didn't make a profit, there'd be no way for them to stay in business. Then, where would customers go to get what they need? Both the business and its customers would be worse off.

    - The opposite of a profit is a loss. This happens when a person or a business is actually losing money instead of earning money. Businesses can't stay open for long if they're losing money.

7. Class Activity: Bring in local businesspersons to speak to the class. Ask them to speak about why they started a business in the first place, what their businesses do, and how they know if they are making a profit or not. You may consider asking a class parent who has started their own business.

Assignment

Come up with a list of up to 10 activities that you do every day. For each activity, brainstorm the various incentives motivating you to complete that activity. For example, you may have to eat all of your dinner every day. Your motivation or incentive for doing so could include any of the following:

- To stop being hungry
- To make your parents happy
- To set a good example for your siblings
- To have dessert
- To enjoy the food

"The Missing Key" Lesson

Chapter 3

Risky Decisions

"John."

"Sarah."

"Brian."

"Striker."

Striker walked over to join his teammates. He was at P.E., and teams were being picked for a game of dodgeball they were about to play. Striker really liked P.E., and dodgeball days were especially exciting.

"Ralph."

"Oh great," thought Striker, as Ralph walked over to the other team. "This should be fun." And sure enough, Ralph immediately turned around and pretended to aim at Striker.

"Courtney."

"Ryan."

"Bill."

Bill jogged over to Striker. "All right!" he said, giving Striker a high five. "I'm ready for some action!" He laughed. "And I hope you're ready to run! Ralph's been glaring at you since we got out here."

"I know," said Striker. "Good thing he's such a bad shot."

The two boys sat back and watched the rest of their classmates be divided into the two teams. Jim Montoya was the last player picked.

"Man," whispered Bill, as Jim ran to join their team, "you know you're bad when your own best friend won't pick you until last."

And it was true. Jim's best friend Zack Marcus was one of the team captains, but still, Jim was the last person picked.

"Yeah," agreed Striker quietly. "I'm not surprised though. Jim's pretty good most of the time, but when he forgets his glasses, he's nothing but a target."

"He forgets his glasses a lot," said Bill.

"I know," said Striker. "I heard his mom yelling at him about it before school one day. It was embarrassing."

The two teams lined up on opposite sides of the gym and picked up the rubber balls. Their P.E. teacher checked to make sure everyone was ready, and then blew his whistle. Pandemonium broke out. Balls were flying everywhere, and Striker was enduring almost a constant stream of balls thrown at him from Ralph. He had to spend so much time jumping out of the way that, for a full five minutes, he didn't get one chance to throw a ball himself.

At one point, Striker jumped out of the way of a fastball thrown by Ralph just in time for it to slam into Jim who had been standing behind him. Without his glasses, Jim didn't even see it coming. "You're out," called the P.E. teacher.

"I know, I know," muttered Jim. "Big surprise." On his way to the sideline, he was hit by several more throws. The balls kept nailing Jim from behind, and then bouncing off every which way. Towards the end, it seemed like he didn't even notice them anymore.

The next morning, Striker arrived at school a little early, so he headed for the playground to kill time before school started. When he reached the playground, he found a big group of kids already gathered. They were all crowded around the basketball court, but he couldn't see what they were looking at. He walked up behind the crowd, when a girl turned around in front of him. It was Sheila.

"Hey, Sheila," said Striker, swallowing hard. "What's going on?"

"Hi, Striker! Someone just got in trouble for walking in the wet concrete."

"What wet concrete?" asked Striker, still trying to see.

"Look," Sheila moved over a little so that Striker could just see through a crack between the people.

Apparently, the floor of the concrete basketball court had been re-laid early that morning, and so now a smooth lake of wet concrete stretched out in front of Striker. Just for a moment, Striker had the itching sensation that he really, really wanted to leave his footprints, or initials, or something, in the fresh concrete that seemed to be waiting just for him. He tried to get a hold on himself, reminding himself just how much trouble he'd be in for leaving his mark.

Finally, Striker took a deep breath and managed to say, "I'm glad they fixed the court. But, what's the problem?"

"Can't you see?" asked Sheila. "Look right over there… by the goal…"

Striker squinted, wishing that there weren't quite so many people in front of him, and finally spied what looked like footprints in the concrete.

"So someone else must have had the same urge I had," thought Striker. "There's just something about wet concrete."

The footprints started at the edge and headed towards the middle for about 5 yards or so. Then, the footprints wandered around in crazy circles as if the person wasn't quite sure where they were going or what they were doing. Finally, the footprints led back out of the middle to the same edge, leaving behind them a trail of ruined concrete.

"Wow," breathed Striker. "Someone's going to get in trouble for that. Didn't they see that huge sign?"

And indeed, there beside the court was a large yellow sign reading "WET CONCRETE-- Stay off the Court!"

"Somebody already has gotten in trouble for it," said Sheila. "And you should have seen Ms. Peters when she caught him—she was as red as a fire truck! I felt so bad for Jim!"

"Jim?" thought Striker. "Uh oh. I hope it wasn't Jim Montoya."

But sure enough, right then he saw Jim walking out of the school building, with an angry-looking Ms. Peters behind him. He was barefoot and was holding his gym shoes in his hand.

"Now put your extra shoes on," said Ms. Peters. "And I don't want to hear that you've even looked at that basketball court, understand?"

"Yes, ma'am," said Jim quietly.

Ms. Peters turned and stalked back to the building.

Just then, Bill came up behind Striker and Sheila. "Hey, guys, what's going on?"

Striker filled him in.

"Whoa," said Bill. "I'm gonna go ask Jim why he's not in more trouble or something. I'm surprised they're letting him back out on the playground!"

Bill ran over to Jim, had a quick conversation, and then hurried back.

"Of all the luck!" exclaimed Bill. "Guess why Jim's not in trouble?"

"I dunno," said Sheila.

"Why?" asked Striker.

"Because he forgot his glasses!"

"What does that have to do with it?" asked Sheila.

"Don't you get it? Jim couldn't read the sign! He didn't even know the concrete was wet. He was halfway across the court before he realized that something was sticking to his shoes!"

"And so he didn't get in trouble?" said Sheila.

"How could he?" asked Bill. "I mean, he should have had his glasses with him, but otherwise, it wasn't really his fault."

"Man," said Striker. "He *is* lucky."

That day at P.E., they were again about to start a game of dodgeball. They had the same two captains from the day before.

"I wish I could be a captain," Bill complained to Striker as the teams started being picked. "How come they always get to do it?"

"Oh, come on," said Striker. "You know it goes by weeks. Maybe you'll get to be one next week."

"But we'll be playing badminton next week. That's not as important as dodgeball!"

Striker laughed.

They had been so busy talking that they hadn't been paying attention to the names being called out

"Striker!" said Mr. Adams. "Your name was just called. Go join your team." He gestured to Zack's team.

"Sorry," said Striker, hurrying to his team. He joined the group, taking his place by Jim.

"Wait a minute," thought Striker. "Jim?"

He turned to check again, and sure enough, there was Jim standing next to him, already on the team.

"Jim," started Striker, "not to be rude or anything…but what are you doing here?"

"What do you mean?" asked Jim. "Zack picked me. He is my best friend, you know."

"I know…" said Striker, "But… when did he pick you?"

"First," said Jim.

"Really?" asked Striker before he could stop himself.

Jim shrugged. "I guess he decided to take a chance on me today."

Striker had a perplexed look on his face that Jim couldn't help but notice.

"What's wrong?" he asked.

Striker was quiet for a second, and then said, "You walked across that concrete this morning on purpose, didn't you?"

How did Striker know?

Solution

People take risks all the time, but they want to balance those risks with whether or not they think they'll pay off in the end. If people don't think a risk will pay off, they generally don't take it. That's why Jim's best friend Zack wouldn't pick Jim for his team whenever Jim forgot his glasses. Without his glasses, Jim just wouldn't play well, so Zack would always pick someone else first. Jim was a bad risk.

That's why when Zack suddenly did pick Jim first, Striker knew that something had changed. Either Zack didn't care about taking a bad risk anymore, which was unlikely, or Jim was no longer a bad risk. Zack must have known that Jim was somehow able to play well, even without his glasses.

If Jim could play well without his glasses, that led Striker to the most obvious conclusion: Jim had contacts. And if Jim had contacts, that meant that he could have read the "WET CONCRETE" sign that morning.

When Striker explained all this to Jim, Jim reluctantly admitted that he was right.

"But I didn't mean to walk across the concrete." Jim told Striker, "I just couldn't help it! It was calling to me… And after I did it, the only way I could get out of trouble was by pretending I couldn't see the sign. You've got to understand!"

Fortunately for Jim, Striker understood all too well the lure of wet concrete.

"I won't tell on you," said Striker, "but only on two conditions. First, that in a couple of days, you'll tell everyone you got contacts. Don't keep hiding it, or you might be tempted to do something else."

Jim nodded.

"And second…"

After the dodgeball game that afternoon, everyone was talking about how badly Jim had played.

"Jim was terrible! I mean, he certainly did throw a lot of balls, but they were all at his own teammate!"

"Yeah, I know. I've never seen anything like it!"

"He must have tagged him about 25 times!"

"Probably more than that! Poor Ralph… He never knew what hit him."

Striker Jones, "Risky Decisions"

Lesson Plan

Objective: Students will be able to explain and apply the economic concept of balancing risks against benefits.

Procedure

1. Read the chapter "Risky Decisions" up until the Solution, either as a class or separately.

2. In pairs or small groups, have students discuss what they believe is the solution to the mystery.

3. Read the Solution as a class.

4. As a class, define the word *risk* (exposure to possibly losing something). Review the word *benefit* (something that is good).

5. Check for understanding with the following questions:

    - In the beginning of the story, why wouldn't Zack pick Jim for his team? (Jim had forgotten his glasses and likely wouldn't play well.)

    - At the end of the story, Zack finally does pick Jim for his team. How is his decision less risky than if he'd picked him at the beginning of the story? (Zack knows that Jim has contacts and can actually see just fine. So, he expects picking Jim will now pay off because he will have a good player on his team who can see well.)

- Did Zack's decision pay off? (Not this time. We find out that Jim played very poorly in the last match of dodgeball. He spent the entire time throwing at his teammate, Ralph!)

6. Discuss the concepts of risks and benefits. Key points include the following:

    - When we're doing something we shouldn't be doing, it's easy to think of the risk involved. For instance, if you play on the computer at night when you should be in bed, you're running the risk that your parents will catch you. But in fact, every decision we make every day has some element of risk in it, even when we're deciding whether or not to do something nice. For instance, if you're friendly to the new student in class, you're running the risk that he/she might be mean in return.

    - Risk isn't all bad. Instead, it can make us more careful about the decisions that we make. Knowing that a risk is involved helps people think through all the consequences of their actions.

    - The key is to balance potential risks with potential benefits. If the possible benefit of an activity is greater than the possible risk, then we say the benefits outweigh the risks, and the activity is probably worth doing. So, though you may run a risk that the new kid in class could be mean to you, the possible benefit is that you make a new friend! Does that benefit outweigh the risk?

7. Class Activity: With the class, come up with a list of up to 10 common daily activities. For each activity, brainstorm the various risks and benefits involved in completing that activity. Then, allow students to vote to show whether or not they would do that activity. Example:

Activity: Sharing a toy with a friend

<u>Benefits and risks of sharing</u>	<u>Benefits and risks of not sharing</u>
Risk: We might not get the toy back.	Risk: We might upset our friend.
Benefit: We make our friend happy.	Risk: We might be disappointed in ourselves.
Benefit: We build a stronger friendship.	Benefit: We get to play with the toy ourselves.

Assignment

People have different attitudes towards risk, none of which are better than the others. Some people don't mind risk very much, and they'll take big chances even when there's a big risk of that it won't pay off. Other people don't like risk at all. They tend to stick to easy decisions where there's little chance of losing anything.

Write a paragraph describing where you fall in your feeling about risk. Would you rather risk a lot to gain a lot, or would you rather play it safe and not risk too much, even if it means you might not gain as much? Do you fall somewhere in the middle? Give two examples that demonstrate your own attitude toward risk.

"Risky Decisions" Lesson

Chapter 4

Looks Like Love

"On top of spa-ghet-tiiii," sang Striker.

Amy stopped playing the piano and put her hands to her head. "Whoa, Striker. Hold on."

"What's wrong?" he asked. "I was just getting warmed up."

Amy cleared her throat. "I think we might need to start a little slower. You're not quite ready for belting out songs yet." She scooted the piano bench closer to the instrument. "I'm going to play a note, and then I want you to sing it back to me, ok?"

"Ok," said Striker. "I think I can handle that."

"Well, we'll see," said Amy quietly.

"What was that?" asked Striker.

"Nothing," said Amy. "Ok, here we go."

She pressed down on one of the ivory keys, while Striker sang the note back to her with a "La."

"Ok," she said, "here's another." She pressed one note higher.

Striker cleared his throat before singing out another "La."

Amy nodded her head. "Not bad." She pressed third key one step higher on the keyboard.

"La—" started Striker before his throat seemed to close in on itself, emitting one long, high-pitched squeak.

"Ok!" said Amy, holding up her hands for him to stop. "That one was not so good."

"I know," said Striker. "But I can't seem to help it." He hung his head. "Maybe we shouldn't worry about this. I'll probably never get better."

"Oh, please," said Amy. "I'm not going to give up on you."

"Ok," said Striker with a grimace. "If you say so."

Just then, there was a knock on the door. Striker had been so focused on singing that he had practically forgotten where they were.

Striker and Amy were in the piano practice room at Guy Larson's Piano Paradise. Mr. Larson mainly sold new musical instruments, but he also had a piano practice room that he rented out for an hour at a time to customers. Luckily for Striker and Amy, Striker's dad knew Mr. Larson very well, and so they were allowed to use the practice room for free, so long as they weren't taking the place of any paying customers.

"Uh oh," groaned Striker, "Mr. Larson's probably coming to complain that my singing is driving his customers away."

Amy laughed as she ran to open the door.

"Hi, Mr. Larson," she said sweetly as she opened the door. Striker suspected that Amy might have a bit of a crush on Mr. Larson. He was pretty young (for an adult, anyways), and he'd overheard Amy telling Sheila that he was "super cute."

Mr. Larson stepped into the room, smiling at the kids. "Hey, you two," he said. "I'm afraid I've got to throw you out for a little bit. One of my regulars is here to use the piano room."

"Oh, that's ok," said Amy smiling. "We understand. You've got to take care of your customers first. Besides," she lowered her voice to a half whisper, "Striker's voice is probably in need of a break."

Ignoring Amy, Striker smiled politely at Mr. Larson. "Yeah, we understand," he said. "Thanks for letting us use the room."

"No problem," said Mr. Larson. "Come back whenever you want and see if the room is free."

"Ok!" said Amy brightly. "See you soon!"

Striker followed Amy out of the room, stepping out of the way of a teenager waiting to use the piano.

On their way out the door, Striker accidentally clipped the edge of a cymbal display with his jacket. Several pairs of cymbals toppled from their racks on the wall.

"Sorry," yelled Striker over the loud crashes.

"It's ok," shouted back Mr. Larson. "I'll take care of it!"

Outside on the street, Amy turned to Striker. Now that she wasn't around Mr. Larson, she was once again her businesslike self. "Ok, good practice," she said. "I want you to sing some tonight at home, and we'll come back after school tomorrow, ok?"

"All right," said Striker with a sigh.

"And one more thing," added Amy. "Tomorrow, let's try our best to not knock down the entire store, ok?"

The next morning at school, Striker was once again in music class. He was feeling relatively stress-free, because he knew he wouldn't be picked to do a solo again so soon.

That day, the students were learning how to sing a round. They started with an easy example, "Row Your Boat." Right when Striker's group was getting to "gently down the stream," a delivery boy slipped in and out of the classroom, leaving behind him a large vase of red roses. Slowly, the round died out as each student looked at the bouquet.

"How pretty!" sighed a girl behind Striker.

Ms. Harper walked over to the vase. "Sorry for the interruption, class," she said, pulling the accompanying note from among the flowers. As she read the card, pink started to spread across her cheeks. All the girls in the class let out a sigh as Ms. Harper changed colors. Striker and Bill rolled their eyes.

Ms. Harper set the card down on her desk and walked back to the front of the class. "Ok," she said, "let's try that round again."

"But who are the flowers from?" asked a girl in the front row.

"Don't worry about that," said Ms. Harper with a smile. "You are here to sing, so that's what we're going to do. Ready?"

A general sigh went around the room again, as everyone started their part.

"Row, row, row your boat…"

That day at lunch, everyone was talking about the flowers. More than one head was turned toward the teacher's table, where Ms. Harper sat with a young art teacher named Mr. Wharton.

"I snuck a peak at the note after class," whispered Amy to Bill, Striker, and Sheila.

"What!?" they all exclaimed at once, looking at Amy in amazement.

"What did it say?" Sheila added eagerly.

"'From your secret admirer!'" said Amy with glee. "Isn't that exciting? I wonder who they could have been from."

"They must have been from Mr. Wharton," said Sheila, gesturing towards the teacher's table. "Look at how he's leaning in to hear what she's saying."

"Maybe it's just loud in here," said Bill, taking a spoonful out of his pudding cup. "He probably has to lean over to hear her!"

Sheila shot him a look. "Don't be silly. Obviously, he loves her."

"Oooh, look!" interrupted Amy, pointing back to the teacher's table. Another young male teacher had come to sit on the other side of Ms. Harper. This teacher was Mr. Dasher, a math teacher. "Maybe the flowers were from Mr. Dasher!" said Amy.

"Hmm," said Sheila, thoughtfully, "he's leaning towards her, too. I wonder what it all means…"

"Not to repeat myself," said Bill, "but have I mentioned that it's loud in here?"

Striker laughed, while Amy gave a loud sigh. "Boys know nothing about romance."

That afternoon, Striker was back in the piano room with Amy. She would play five notes in a row, which Striker would then have to sing back to her. Slowly, the notes Striker sang were sounding more and more like the notes that were coming out of the piano.

"That's good, Striker," said Amy. "After a few more lessons, I think you won't be too bad."

"Wow," said Striker, "with encouragement like that, how could I go wrong?"

Amy only smiled and kept playing notes for Striker to repeat. After a few more minutes, Striker stopped her.

"I have got to get some water," he said. "All this singing is making my throat sore."

"Ok," said Amy, "but hurry back. You never know when a paying customer is going to walk in."

"I will," he said, walking out the door of the practice room. Once outside though, he slowed down, secretly thinking that he wouldn't mind calling it a day.

"No need to hurry," he thought. "I can only take so much singing."

Striker ambled toward the front of the store where the water fountain was, but as he neared the fountain, he stopped abruptly. There in the entryway was sitting Ms. Harper, his music teacher, chatting with Mr. Larson.

"They'll be done soon," Mr. Larson was saying. "I let them have the practice room for an hour at a time, so they've got a little longer left."

"Oh, I don't mind waiting," said Ms. Harper.

"Waiting?" thought Striker. Suddenly, he felt very much like he was intruding. Slowly, he crept backwards, trying hard not to be noticed. Unfortunately, on his way backwards, he managed to crash into a display of music stands. As they fell, they made a terrible racket, prompting Striker to turn tail and run in the direction of the piano room. The ringing noises followed him around the corner as he bolted for the practice room door.

He threw himself inside the room and came face to face with a surprised Amy.

"What in the world are you doing?" she asked. She put her hands on her hips. "Mr. Larson's going to throw us out if you keep knocking things over."

"Sorry," he breathed, panting from his sprint. "It's just that Ms. Harper was up front."

"Oh really?" asked Amy. "We should say hi. Maybe we'll get a hint as to who sent her those flowers."

"Amy," said Striker. "Didn't you hear me? Ms. Harper's waiting for the piano room."

"It's so romantic," said Amy, paying little attention to Striker. "Which teacher do you think they were from?"

Striker shook his head. "You're not listening to me." He looked at Amy. "Obviously, they were from Mr. Larson."

How can Striker be so sure?

Solution

When someone owns a business, they have to charge for at least some of their services. That helps them stay in business. So, even though Mr. Larson was very nice and let Striker and Amy use his practice room for free, whenever someone came along who was willing to pay, Mr. Larson would let the paying customer use the room.

But when Ms. Harper came in to use the piano, Mr. Larson didn't kick the kids out of the room. Instead, he told Ms. Harper that the kids would use the practice room for an hour. This made Striker wonder why Mr. Larson wouldn't let Ms. Harper into the room right away like with he did all of his other customers.

Then he got an idea. If Ms. Harper had to wait to use the piano, she would probably wait at the front of the store. And if she were at the front of the store, Mr. Larson would be able to talk to her. And that meant that maybe, just maybe, Mr. Larson liked Ms. Harper.

Striker never did find out if Mr. Larson had sent the flowers or not. However, when Ms. Harper and Mr. Larson got married six months later, he figured that he had probably been right.

At the wedding, Amy shed lots of tears for Mr. Larson. Luckily, though, Mr. Larson's much younger brother was also at the wedding.

It didn't take long for Amy to move on.

Striker Jones, "Looks Like Love"

Lesson Plan

Objective: Students will be able to explain and apply the economic concepts of goods vs. services and opportunity cost.

Procedure

1. Read the chapter "Looks Like Love" up until the Solution, either as a class or separately.

2. In pairs or small groups, have students discuss what they believe is the solution to the mystery.

3. Read the Solution as a class.

4. As a class, define the words *goods* (actual products that you can see and touch), *service* (work performed for others), and *opportunity cost* (the next best thing that you give up when you choose one thing over something else).

5. Check for understanding with the following questions:

    - In the story, Mr. Larsen ran a business. What kind of goods did he provide? (Musical instruments and accessories, such as the cymbals and music stands that Striker knocked over.)

    - What kind of services did he provide? (Providing a place for musicians to practice was a service.)

    - Why did Mr. Larsen sometimes have to ask Amy and Striker to leave the practice room? (He had a paying customer who needed the room. He has to keep customers to keep his business open.)

- Imagine that a paying customer came in to Mr. Larsen's store, and he didn't ask Amy and Striker to leave the practice room. He would have made Amy and Striker happy, but what would he be giving up? That is, what's his opportunity cost? (He would be giving up the rental money for the practice room from a regular customer.)

6. Discuss the concept of goods vs. services and opportunity costs. Key points include the following:

    - Businesses generally provide either goods or services, and sometimes both. A good is a tangible thing, like a bike, a cell phone, or a house. A service is when someone does something for you. So, a teacher is providing a service. So is a fireman, a lawyer, or a nurse.

    - Any time we make any kind of choice, we incur an opportunity cost. This is what we had to give up or what we didn't choose. So, if we choose to play on the swing set, our opportunity cost could be going on the jungle gym. We get to swing, but we don't get to climb the jungle gym. If we choose to go to a birthday party instead of the beach, the beach is our opportunity cost.

    - We incur an opportunity cost no matter whether we're choosing a good or a service. We always have to choose between different alternatives.

7. Class Activity: Set up four stations around the room: two in which an adult helps a student complete a fun activity (though not the same activity at each) and two in which the students

enjoy a particular snack (though not the same snack at each). Give the students 10 minutes at their stations. Afterwards, let students discuss in pairs which station they chose and why; whether it was a good or service that they enjoyed; and what was the opportunity cost involved in their choice. Summarize as a class.

Assignment

Look through a newspaper or magazine and cut out 10 ads: five advertising a good and five advertising a service. Write a short paragraph discussing the difference between the two types of product for sale.

"Looks Like Love" Lesson

Chapter 5

Election Day

One morning, Striker's teacher, Ms. Peters, started out class with an announcement.

"Good morning, students," she said. "Today, we've got something special on our agenda. Each classroom in the entire school is going to send one student to serve on the school's student council."

As a buzz of excited whispers began, Ms. Peters continued. "Now, remember that our student council member will be in charge of coordinating our class's participation in the school fall festival. This means that he or she will be taking on extra responsibilities in addition to class work, so students who aren't serious about the position shouldn't run."

Ms. Peters looked around the classroom. "The election will be held after lunch, but for now, would anyone like to make a nomination?"

Immediately, a girl in the back row shot her hand up.

"Yes, Susan?"

"I nominate Andrew Shoemaker."

Striker silently nodded in agreement. Andrew Shoemaker was studious, responsible, and serious, but was universally liked because of his friendly manner. He was also very humble, which made everyone like him even more. He'd be perfect to represent the class.

"Andrew would be a great choice," thought Striker, and, by the amount of nodding going on around him, he could tell that most of the class was thinking the same thing.

Ms. Peters smiled. "Andrew, do you accept the nomination?"

Andrew nodded, looking a little embarrassed.

"Are there any other nominations?" asked Ms. Peters.

Somehow, Striker didn't think any one else would volunteer. They'd almost definitely lose.

Bill leaned over to Striker. "Only an idiot would run against Andrew," he whispered.

Just then, Ralph raised his hand. "Ms. Peters, I'd like to nominate myself."

Striker looked back at Bill. "Yep. An idiot."

At lunch, Striker sat watching Andrew Shoemaker at a nearby table. Andrew was normally relaxed and friendly, but today he was nervously shredding his napkin instead of eating and laughing as usual. Ralph, on the other hand, looked downright cocky. Striker watched him walking from table to table, speaking to different students.

"He's probably campaigning," thought Striker, before turning his attention back to his table.

"Man, that math test was tough," Bill was saying.

"I didn't think it was too bad," said Amy.

"Did you study for it?" asked Bill.

"Of course," replied Amy.

"Well, that's explains it," he said with a shrug. "You studied. That's like cheating."

Amy rolled her eyes.

"Speaking of cheating," said Sheila, "has anyone else noticed Ralph? He's been very busy talking to students—he hasn't even eaten his lunch."

"Yeah," said Striker. "I was wondering about that myself."

"You don't think he's cheating somehow, do you?" asked Sheila.

"How could he?" asked Amy. "He can't control how people vote."

"That's true," said Striker, "but he could influence them."

Striker noticed that Andrew's eyes had also been following Ralph's movements.

"I think Andrew's wondering the same thing we are," he said out loud.

"Well," said Bill after a moment, "at least Ralph's got enough sense to not come over to our table."

Back in the classroom after lunch, Amy stopped by Striker's seat on the way back to her desk.

"Striker, listen to what I just found out in the girls' bathroom."

Bill leaned in from across the aisle so that he could also hear Amy's whisper.

"Ralph's been promising everyone that if they vote for him, they can go swimming in his pool whenever they want," she said.

"Oh, great" said Striker with a frown. "I hope that doesn't influence too many people."

"Don't worry," said Amy. "The girls I overheard all said they still wouldn't vote for him. No one wants Ralph to represent the class."

"I bet lots of people feel that way," said Bill. "Ralph might have a pool, but that's not enough for people to elect him. Besides, if he was in charge of our class's contribution to the fall festival, we'd probably all end up being the designated gum scrapers or something."

Striker was about to respond when Ms. Peters again stood up at the front of the class. Amy hurried to her seat.

"Ok, class," said Ms. Peters. "It's time to vote for our student council member." She walked down the rows of desks, passing out small pieces of paper. "Write the name of either Andrew or Ralph, fold it up, and then bring it up to my desk."

As the students began writing, Striker carefully wrote out "Andrew Shoemaker," and then folded his piece of paper in half. He walked up with the crowd of other students and dropped his vote into a bowl Ms. Peters had set out on her desk.

After all the names had been collected, Ms. Peters instructed the students to read a chapter in their literature textbooks while she counted the votes.

After a few minutes of unfolding the papers and making tally marks in her notebook, Ms. Peters stood up and made the announcement.

"Judging from your votes," she said, "our new student council representative will be Ralph Johnson."

Gasps went up all around the room.

When Striker and Bill walked outside to recess that day, they ran into what could only be described as an angry mob. About fifteen students were standing in a group complaining heatedly about the election.

"I can't believe Ralph won!"

"Who would have voted for him?"

"Did you see that smug look on his face?"

"I still can't believe it!"

"Andrew should have won!"

"Yeah! Andrew should have won!"

"Whoa," said Bill. "It looks like people aren't happy with the way the election turned out."

"I guess not," said Striker, looking into the sea of angry faces. He spotted Andrew sitting alone at the swing set.

"Let's go talk to Andrew," said Striker. "He doesn't look so good."

Bill and Striker walked over to where Andrew was slowly swinging back and forth, staring down into his lap.

"Hey, Andrew," said Striker and Bill together.

"Hey, guys," said Andrew, still looking down.

"We're sorry about the election," said Bill.

Andrew looked up and sighed. "Oh, that's ok. I can handle losing." He dug his heels into the ground, and the swing slowed to a halt. Then Andrew shrugged his shoulders. "I just don't understand *why* I lost." He pointed over to the group of people. "I mean, look at them! That's almost the whole class, and obviously, none of them wanted Ralph to win. So, what happened?"

"Ralph was promising kids that they could swim in his pool if they voted for him," Bill told Andrew.

"I knew about that," said Andrew, "but it seems like people still really didn't want Ralph to win. I didn't think the chance to go swimming would be enough to change their minds about that."

"It wasn't," said Striker.

Andrew turned to him. "Then what happened? How did Ralph get elected, when no one wanted him to win?"

"I agree with you that no one wanted Ralph to win," said Striker, "but that doesn't change the fact that they all voted for him anyway."

Why did everyone vote for Ralph?

Solution

Little choices lead to big outcomes. People first make individual choices based on what's best for themselves, and lots of times, these little decisions then lead to great results. For example, when all the people on a street decide to clean up their own yards, the entire neighborhood looks nice.

However, when lots of people make little choices, it can sometimes lead to one big outcome that no one wants. For instance, someone might decide not to give money to charity, because the little amount they could give wouldn't really make much of a difference. But if everyone thinks that way, then no one would give to charity, and then suddenly, charities wouldn't have any money at all!

The same thing happened in the class election. No one wanted Ralph to win. But everybody did want to vote for him so that they could go swimming in his pool. Plus, everyone thought it would be ok to vote for Ralph, because their one vote couldn't possibly be enough to elect him. But with everyone thinking that, everyone voted for Ralph, and Ralph won.

Striker felt pretty bad explaining to Andrew why he had lost, but Andrew managed to take it in stride. As Andrew walked away, Striker couldn't but help think again what a good student council member Andrew would have made.

Bill, however, did not take it as well as Andrew. For weeks, he maintained that there should be some way to punish the students who had foolishly voted for Ralph.

Then the fall festival finally rolled around, when it was discovered that Ralph had forgotten to go to all the planning meetings. After a last-minute scramble to find jobs for the class, the principal placed Striker and his classmates in charge of running the coatroom. As they glumly watched kids from other classrooms work the dunking booth and the haunted house, Bill decided everyone had probably received enough punishment.

Striker Jones, "Election Day"

Lesson Plan

Objective: Students will be able to explain and apply the economic concept of public choice theory, though we will refer to it with students as decision-making in groups.

Procedure

1. Read the chapter "Election Day" up until the Solution, either as a class or separately.

2. In pairs or small groups, have students discuss what they believe is the solution to the mystery.

3. Read the Solution as a class.

4. Check for understanding with the following questions:

    - Did most students want Ralph to win the election? How do we know? (No. They were angry at the outcome.)

    - Did most students vote for Ralph? How do we know? (Yes. Ralph won the election, so he must have had most of the votes.)

    - Why did people vote for Ralph? (Ralph promised that everyone who voted for him could swim in his pool. Each person wanted this benefit, while thinking that his/her one vote couldn't possibly be enough to make Ralph win.)

5. Discuss the concept of decision-making in groups. Key points include the following:

- When people are not held directly responsible for the consequences of their actions, you can get bad results. For instance, when no one thought that their vote would really count, or could be enough to turn the tide, they were happy to vote in their own best interests, rather than in the best interests of the group. This happens quite a bit in group decision-making. The bigger the group, the more likely it is to happen. In this case, little decisions add up to one bad outcome.

- Luckily, lots of people making individual decisions can also add up to some wonderful outcomes, as long as each person is responsible for his own actions. For instance, every time you go to the store, you're getting the benefit of hundreds or even thousands of people all working together. They're each playing their part by working to take care of themselves. Yet, all of that individual activity combines to create one amazing store where you can go to buy all kinds of things!

- The difference in whether you get a good outcome or a bad outcome depends on whether people are held directly responsible for their decisions. When people can hide in a group, it's much harder to hold people responsible. On the other hand, when they're working in a business or as an individual, they can't hide as easily and are held directly responsible for their actions. As a result, they make better choices. Lots of these little good choices all add up to one big positive outcome!

Class Activity/Assignment

Recreate the student council election from the chapter. Have one child play Ralph and one child play Andrew. Allow each to give a speech to the class about how they would serve as student council representative. Hold the election and tally the votes. Discuss as a class how the election results differed from the chapter, if at all, and why. Then, have each student write a paragraph describing how he/she voted, why, and what effect his/her vote had on the entire class.

"Election Day" Lesson

Chapter 6

Smarts and Crafts

It was the day before Christmas vacation, and the kids in Striker's class were getting antsy. As they walked back into the classroom from lunch, everyone was chattering.

"I wish it was time to go home," sighed Sheila.

"I know," said Striker. "This afternoon's going to be torture!"

There was general agreement from several students around them, as everyone dropped into their seats. Work was clearly the last thing on anyone's mind. Bill and Zack began to knock a paper football around while Sheila texted under her desk. Ralph was flipping through a comic book, and even Andrew was passing notes.

Ms. Peters strode to the front of the classroom and knocked on the white board.

"Earth to students," she said with a smile. "I know we're all gearing up for vacation, but we're not there yet! We've got a fun project we're going to work on this afternoon. Everyone is going to make a fleece scarf!"

"A scarf?" Striker heard Ralph mutter. "Why would I want to make one of those?"

Sheila clearly felt differently. "How fun! I love to design clothes. Mine is going to be gorgeous!"

"Not so fast," continued Ms. Peters over the growing noise from the students. "We're not going to get to keep them. Instead we're going to donate them to the Chorale Pals, our local community chorus. They are going caroling at the local nursing home over the break, and we are going to support them by donating scarves for them to wear while singing."

The spark of interest from the students abruptly faded.

"We have to make scarves, and we don't even get to keep them?" asked Ralph.

"Hey," whispered Sheila to Amy, "Aren't you in the Chorale Pals?"

Amy nodded. "I joined it when we first moved here."

"Come on, guys," said Ms. Peters loudly, frowning at the lukewarm response. "Where is your holiday spirit? Now," she clapped her hands, "supplies are at the front of the class, and I've got several different colors of material. You need to cut out your scarf, and then use the other colors to make patterns. You can use the fabric glue I've provided to attach your designs."

"Come on!" said Sheila, considerably more energized than any other student. She grabbed Amy's hand and pulled her to the front of the room. They reached the materials before anyone else and began to rummage around.

Striker watched them from his seat as other students meandered to the materials table.

"Man," said Bill beside him. "I'm glad we're not doing regular work, but I could think of a hundred things to do that would be more fun than making a scarf. Why can't this morning's Christmas party just go all day?"

"Yeah," said Striker. "But at least we've got the party candy to keep us going!" He pulled out his goody bag from the class Christmas party. It was overflowing with sweets.

Bill stole a chocolate and pointed to the front of the room. Sheila was excitedly comparing gold and red material at the supplies table. "Sheila's scarf is probably going to be the only good one."

Striker looked around at the other students. Sheila did seem to be the only person who was enthusiastic about the project.

"Hey," he said to Bill. "Let's make a little bet."

Bill leaned forward and raised his eyebrows.

Striker continued. "I'm going to go out on a limb and guess that Sheila's scarf isn't the best one—but don't tell her I said that," he added quickly.

"Really?" asked Bill. "Ok, then, I'll bite. Whose do you think it will be?"

"Amy's," said Striker.

Bill laughed out loud. "Amy?" He glanced to the front of the room where Amy stood with an exasperated look on her face as Sheila held up a swatch of royal blue fabric against her. "Amy doesn't look like she's too into the project. You're on!"

Striker grinned. "Ok. What are we betting?"

Bill looked thoughtful. "Hmm… If I win, you give me your candy."

"Ok," said Striker. "But if I win, I get yours."

Bill laughed. "Deal."

The boys shook hands.

"Now, stop taking my chocolate," said Striker. "You've got a scarf to make."

They left their desks to pick out their materials.

One hour later, the classroom was in shambles. Scraps of materials were strewn everywhere. Glue was dripping off the edges of several desks. Unbeknownst to him, Ralph had a red fleece triangle glued to the side of his head. More students were talking than working.

Striker's own scarf wasn't much to look at. He'd tried to work in some Christmas spirit, but all of his fleece Christmas trees turned out as rectangles. The toy soldier he'd tried to fashion looked like a robot.

"Oh, well," he thought. "Robots probably celebrate Christmas, too."

Even Sheila had lost steam. She had started with very grandiose plans, but somewhere along the way, she'd been sidetracked by talking with another girl about her Christmas plans. Now, she was surrounded by ten different colors of fleece with dozens of cutout pieces littered across her desk.

She noticed Striker watching her and smiled.

"I think I bit off more than I can chew," she said.

Striker laughed.

"Keep it down, guys," said an irritated voice. Striker and Sheila turned in surprise to look at Amy. She was putting the finishing touches on her scarf.

Striker and Bill had been watching her with interest for the past hour. (Striker reflected that this was probably why they'd gotten so little work done on their own scarves.) Amy had been working very diligently on her scarf. Once she'd helped Sheila pick out materials, she had selected a few colors of her own and returned to her seat, where she worked quietly for the entire hour. Now, she had a pretty, snowy white scarf with a pattern of blue and purple snowflakes scattered across the ends. It wasn't a masterpiece, but it was the best in the class.

Bill had been observing Amy with mounting amazement. Now, he shook his head slowly, looking from Amy's scarf to Sheila's mess.

"I don't know how you predicted that," he whispered to Striker. "But I've got a funny feeling that I have to say goodbye to my goody bag."

"Don't worry," said Striker, snagging the bag from Bill's desk. "I'll find a good home for it."

How did Striker know?

Solution

It's difficult to work hard on something if you know it's just going to be taken away from you, even if it is for a good cause. For that reason, we all put more effort into things that we own ourselves. We know we will reap the benefits of our work.

So, when the class heard that the scarves would all be donated, most decided not to give the project their best effort. Even Sheila, who enjoyed fashion design so much, was unable to keep up her enthusiasm. She spent most of the time talking with a neighbor about the upcoming Christmas vacation rather than working on the scarf that she would never be able to wear herself.

However, one person in the class would be able to benefit from the project—the student who was actually in the Chorale Pals. As a chorus member, Amy would be able to keep her scarf and wear it while caroling at the nursing home. Since she would be able to reap the benefits of her own work, Striker knew that she had good reason to put in more effort and make a scarf she could be proud of. And that's exactly what happened.

Striker walked home that afternoon munching on Bill's candy. He'd graciously allowed Bill to keep the caramels, but he'd insisted on keeping all the chocolate himself.

It was going to be a good holiday.

Striker Jones, "Smarts and Crafts"

Lesson Plan

Objective: Students will be able to explain and apply the economic concept of private property rights and incentives.

Procedure

1. Read the chapter "Smarts and Crafts" up until the Solution, either as a class or separately.

2. In pairs or small groups, have students discuss what they believe is the solution to the mystery.

3. Read the Solution as a class.

4. As a class, define the words *private property* (something you own) and *right* (something to which you're entitled). Review the word *incentive* (a factor that motivates behavior).

5. Check for understanding with the following questions:

    - In the story, the class wasn't very enthusiastic about making the scarves. Why? (It was right before Christmas vacation, and they didn't feel like working after the party. They also would not be able to keep the scarves themselves.)

    - Why did Amy work so hard on her scarf? (Amy was in the Chorale Pals, so she would be able to keep her scarf and wear it herself.)

6. Discuss the concept of private property rights. Key points include the following:

   - People have a right to enjoy the fruits of their labor. If you work hard on something, you should reap the benefits. For instance, when parents have jobs, they are paid for their efforts. That's how they enjoy the benefits of their labor. It wouldn't make much sense if your neighbor was paid when your mom went to work, would it?

   - Even when it's for a good cause, people still tend to work harder when they will enjoy the results themselves. In other words, they have more incentive to work hard when they will benefit themselves.

   - Private property rights protect a person's ability to benefit from their own work. If your parents put lots of effort into renovating your house, no one will come along and take it from them. They have private property rights.

   - Many people still donate their time and efforts to charitable causes, even though they may not directly benefit themselves. People work hardest for others, however, when they are freely choosing to do so, not when someone else is making them.

7. Class Activity: Have each student write a paragraph about his/her favorite possession and how he/she would feel if someone stole it. Read some or all of the paragraphs out loud in class. Afterwards, discuss as a class whether it would be right to take away each other's possessions, either for selfish reasons or for a good cause.

Assignment

Interview an adult family member about their work. Why do they have a job? What are the benefits of working besides being paid? How would he/she feel about going to work every day if those benefits were taken away?

"Smarts and Crafts" Lesson

Chapter 7

Auction Action

Striker's school was putting on a charity auction to help the homeless. Each grade had two volunteers to help collect donations and organize the auction, and Striker and Bill were the volunteers from their grade.

One Wednesday in the middle of the collection drive, Striker was halfway through a book report when he was interrupted by a special announcement over the intercom.

"Attention, students," they heard the principal's voice say, "I'm very sorry to announce that we have had a robbery. Someone has stolen the money we collected to donate to the homeless shelter. If anyone has any information about this, please speak to your teacher immediately. We are offering a $20 reward to whoever helps us locate the money."

Striker looked across the aisle at Bill. They each seemed to be asking the same thing. Who would steal from the homeless?

For the rest of the school day, the robbery was all the students could talk about. Everyone was speculating on who could have done it, and what had happened to the money.

"Maybe a teacher took it," said Bill.

"Nah, why would a teacher do that?" said Amy. "It was probably a student. Kids never have any money."

"Maybe someone came in from outside the school. It wouldn't seem so bad if it was a stranger who took it," said Sheila.

All the students in the school had volunteered to be searched. All the desks and backpacks were checked too, and still the money was missing.

After lunch, Striker and Bill were excused from class to help collect the items donated to the charity auction. Each classroom had a box that the students had been filling with donations.

"Excuse me, sir," said Striker, entering one classroom. "I'm here to collect the charity auction donations."

"Oh, certainly," said the teacher. "But I thought the boxes weren't going to be collected until tomorrow."

"Well," answered Striker, "the principal thought that, after the robbery, maybe it would be best to go ahead and collect the items now. That way they'll be in a safe place until the auction on Saturday."

"Ah," said the teacher. "Good idea."

Striker and Bill collected boxes for about an hour, going to every classroom in their grade and delivering the boxes to an empty classroom. After the work was done, the principal locked the door behind them and sent the two boys back to class.

On their way back to class, Bill said, "Well, at least no one can reach that stuff."

"Yeah," agreed Striker. "I can't believe the money's gone, but it would be twice as bad if all the donations for the auction disappeared, too."

The next day after school, Striker and Bill stayed behind to sort through their grade's donations. It was their job to categorize the items.

"Man," said Bill, looking at the pile of donations. "We might be here a little while. What a lot of stuff."

"Yeah," agreed Striker. "I don't think Ms. Peters expected us to get this many donations. We should find some other people to help."

"Yeah," teased Bill, "Maybe we could convince *Sheila* to come help us."

Striker turned red. "I don't know what you're talking about."

"Sure," said Bill laughing.

"Never mind," said Striker, turning redder still. "Just help me with these boxes."

They sat down and began sorting through the items.

"Let's make separate piles," suggested Striker. "We can put clothing here, books and magazines in the corner, artwork on the table, and videos and DVDs under the blackboard."

"Fine by me," said Bill. "But what exactly should we do with things like this?"

He held up what seemed to be a large rubber band.

"I think that's for exercising," said Striker doubtfully. "You stretch it between your arms."

"Like this?" asked Bill, stretching the rubber band across his chest.

"Be careful," warned Striker a moment too late. Bill had not been quite strong enough to stretch the band as far as he did. The rubber band flew out of his right hand and shot across the room straight at Striker.

"Whoa!" shouted Striker, diving out of the way and crashing into the pile of boxes. The rubber band just missed Striker's feet as they flew sideways.

"Sorry!" said Bill when Striker had landed. "Are you ok?"

Striker was quiet for a moment. "Let's make one more pile—crazy and dangerous items. By the pencil sharpener."

After about 30 minutes of working, Striker called out, "Hey, cool!" He had just unearthed a large cowboy hat and was strutting around the room with it on his head.

Bill laughed. "Yeah, well look at this!" He had found a shaggy blue wig. He put it on, shaking it back and forth like a rock star. Striker laughed.

The two boys eventually set back down to work, but continued wearing their new headgear. They worked hard, sometimes talking, sometimes not. The big general pile was slowly getting smaller.

Suddenly, Striker heard Bill give a sharp gasp. "What is it?" he asked.

"Striker, look at this!" Billy had an orange pencil box sitting open in his lap. When he tilted it so that Striker could see inside, Striker too gasped. Inside the box was a large pile of money. They dumped the money on the floor and together counted $250!

"That must be the stolen charity money!" exclaimed Striker.

"But why was it in with the donations?" asked Bill.

"Maybe whoever took it was trying to hide it for a little while. Remember, everybody was volunteering to be searched, so the thief couldn't have kept it on himself."

"But putting it with the donations doesn't seem so smart, either," said Bill. "Now we have it!"

"Yes, but they didn't know we'd have it, did they? We picked up the boxes a day early," replied Striker.

"Wow. Well, I'm glad we've got the money back now. The principal will be really happy about that. Though it's too bad we'll never know who actually took it in the first place."

"Maybe we can find out," said Striker. "Just maybe…"

Two days later, the auction was in full swing. Most of the school kids had turned up with their parents to take part in the bidding. Striker sat near the back. He wanted to be able to see his fellow bidders.

Several items were auctioned off before it got to the item Striker was most interested in. When the orange pencil box was brought out on stage, he sat up as straight as he could and got ready to bid.

The bidding began at ten cents.

"10 cents," said a boy Striker recognized from another classroom named Josh McMillan.

"25 cents," called a girl from Striker's class, Jane Lincoln.

"50 cents," shouted Zack Marcus.

"One dollar," shouted Josh again.

"$1.50," called a new bidder, and "$2.50," shouted yet another bidder.

As the bidding continued up to $5, Striker silently wondered which person in the room was the culprit. Several people were now fighting over the box. When the pencil box hit $6, though, several bidders began to drop out. Unfortunately, not enough people dropped out to give Striker a clear view of what he needed to know. He decided it was time for a drastic move.

"Thirty dollars," he bid loudly.

A murmur went through the crowd. He could see people turning to get a look at the boy who had bid so much for such a small pencil box. His own mother sitting next to him turned to him with a very surprised look on her face.

"Thirty dollars?" she whispered. "What on earth are you doing?"

"Trust me," Striker whispered back.

She gave Striker a concerned look, but said nothing.

The auctioneer, who had stopped momentarily out of surprise, suddenly seemed to remember himself. "The bid is at thirty dollars," he said.

No one spoke. Striker sat waiting. He was sure his plan would work.

"Thirty dollars going once."

Striker squirmed ever so slightly in his seat. He certainly hoped his plan was going to work.

"Thirty dollars going twice."

Striker was getting a little worried, and his mother looked downright alarmed. Now that he thought about it, thirty dollars was a lot of money. And it looked like he might have to pay it after all…

"Come on," thought Striker. "Come on…"

"So—" started the auctioneer, until he was cut off by the cry of another boy a few rows ahead of Striker. It was Josh McMillan.

"Thirty-one!" shouted Josh.

Breathing a quick sigh of relief, Striker was instantly on his feet. "That's him!" he cried to the principal. "Josh must have stolen the money!"

How did Striker know?

Solution

Striker knew that the only way to discover the culprit was to get him to expose himself. By keeping the pencil box in the auction, he was able to do just that. He knew that only the thief expected the pencil box to be filled with money, and so only the thief would be willing to pay a very high price to buy it back. After all, everyone else simply thought it was a nice, but ordinary, orange pencil box. They might be willing to pay $5 or so, but only the thief would be willing to pay a large amount like $31.

Striker and Bill took the $20 reward money and bought two items from the charity auction. As they walked home that evening, they were a very conspicuous pair—one boy swaggering in an enormous cowboy hat and the other bouncing along in a shiny, electric blue wig.

Striker Jones, "Auction Action"

Lesson Plan

Objective: Students will be able to explain and apply the economic concept of information asymmetry, or unequal information.

Procedure

1. Read the chapter "Auction Action" up until the Solution, either as a class or separately.

2. In pairs or small groups, have students discuss what they believe is the solution to the mystery.

3. Read the Solution as a class.

4. As a class, define the words *information* (knowledge that we possess) and *asymmetry* (unequal or out of balance).

5. Check for understanding with the following questions:

    - What special information did Striker have about the pencil box? (He knew that money had been hidden inside of it.)

    - If someone else knew this, would they think the pencil box was more or less valuable than everybody else? (More valuable.)

    - Why wouldn't most people pay $30 for the pencil box? (The pencil box by itself wasn't worth that. They didn't know there might be money inside.)

- How does Striker know who stole the money? (He knew that only one other person would value the pencil box so highly—the thief who thought there was money inside.)

6. Discuss the concept of information asymmetry. Key points include the following:

    - Information asymmetry simply means that one person knows more than the other about something. We experience this all the time. Your teacher probably knows more about world history than you do. You know more about your own family than your teacher does. Thus, you can see, information asymmetry isn't necessarily bad. It's just the way things are.

    - Information asymmetry is important to remember when two people are making a deal of some kind. For instance, if a person is selling a car, he/she will know lots more about the car than a potential buyer. He/she may know good things, like how well the car runs in the cold, or bad things, like sometimes the car doesn't start! In that case, the buyer would either expect the seller to share those important pieces of information or could do research on his/her own to learn more about the car.

    - Information asymmetry can also affect multiple people who are thinking about buying the same thing, as is the case with the pencil box in the story. Someone may have special knowledge about the product to think it's more valuable, or maybe even less valuable, than everybody else thinks it is.

7. Class Activity: With the class, examine the role that information plays in how we value something. Show the class some sort of good or service for sale, and decide as a group a fair price for it. Then, introduce additional pieces of information about that good or service, and discuss with the class how the new information affects how they value it. Include both ordinary and outlandish examples. For example:

   <u>Item for sale: Scuba diving lessons</u>

   Let the class pick a price for the lessons.

   - What if the scuba diving lessons were with LeBron James? Would the value go up or down to you? (Up, because you'd get to meet LeBron James.)

   - What if the lessons didn't include the scuba gear? Value up or down? (Down, because you'd have to buy or rent the equipment yourself.)

   - What if the lessons were in Antarctica? Value up or down? (Down, because you'd be so cold! Or maybe up, if you've always wanted to see penguins!)

   Repeat with a few different goods or services.

Assignment

With the Internet, it's much easier now for people to balance out information asymmetry. There's so much knowledge available online that people can do their own research and learn quite a bit, even if they're not experts in a particular area. This is especially helpful when people are planning to make a big purchase, like a house, a car, or an appliance.

Interview an adult family member about the last big purchase he/she made. Did he/she do any independent research on his/her own before buying? Did he/she use a salesperson to get information? Did he/she use the Internet or consumer guides? How did he/she balance out the information asymmetry?

Chapter 8

The Egg Hunt Hoodwink

It was Easter, and the Johnsons were throwing their annual Easter egg hunt for all the neighborhood kids. Striker met Bill at the corner of his street, and they walked over together.

"Man, I just love egg hunts," said Bill as they neared the Johnson's. "Every year the competition gets fiercer, but this year I'm ready." He pointed to his shoes.

"Bill," asked Striker, stifling a laugh, "are those track shoes?"

"They sure are," said Bill. "Ralph is not out-hunting me this year. I'm prepared. Look, they've even got little spikes on them. Those are for improved traction."

"Very impressive," said Striker laughing. "I'm sure Mrs. Johnson will appreciate you poking holes all over her yard."

"Well, that's the price you pay for hosting an egg hunt. This is war, Striker."

They reached the front door and rang the doorbell. When the door was opened by Mrs. Johnson and her son Ralph, they walked inside, giving polite hellos to Mrs. Johnson and nods to Ralph. Both Bill's and Striker's moms had made them promise to be nice.

"Hopefully, a nod is nice enough for one day," thought Striker.

"Hello, boys," said Mrs. Johnson. "Just go through to the backyard. That's where everyone is."

By then, the party was in full swing. Mrs. Johnson had made lots of cookies and brownies, and Mr. Johnson had whipped up a batch of his special wildberry punch that the kids all looked forward to every year. When Striker stepped out through the back door, the first person he noticed was Sheila. She was wearing a sundress, and he felt the stomach butterflies starting up immediately. Luckily, he was immediately distracted as Mrs. Johnson announced that it was time to begin. Striker joined the other kids scrambling for a basket to collect their eggs.

Once everyone had found a basket, they lined up along the back porch, waiting for the signal to start hunting. Striker looked to his left and let out a laugh when he saw Bill. Bill had taken a red bandana out of his pocket and tied it around his head.

"Psst, Bill," whispered Striker. "Are you sure you don't want any smoke bombs or hand grenades?"

"We'll see who's laughing when this is all over, and I have all the eggs," replied Bill, taking a runner's stance as at the start of a race.

"Hey!" someone called. "Ralph doesn't have a basket."

"Oh, that's ok," said Mrs. Johnson. "Ralph wanted to help hide the eggs, so he won't be playing this year."

"Ok, everybody ready?" asked Mr. Johnson.

"Yeah!" was the reply. Bill was especially loud.

"Then ready…set…GO!" he shouted.

Everyone took off in different directions, causing many kids to crash into each other and fall to the ground. Striker ran for the hedges. On his way, he had to dodge two kids whose crash had landed them in the Johnson's pool and then vault over one boy who'd managed to trip and fall over all by himself. Once he'd reached the bushes, Striker started to search among the leaves.

"Yes!" he shouted as he found a bright green egg. He opened it and found a chocolate candy inside.

"Good job, Striker," said Sheila, gliding past behind him.

Striker felt his face turn red. Wiping his forehead, he decided to dash to the punch table for a quick drink to cool off.

At the punch table, Mr. Johnson was doling out cups of the tasty liquid while Ralph stood next to him drinking a tall glass of his own. "Mmm mmm," Ralph practically shouted to Striker. "This punch sure is good! I love wildberry!"

"Um… that's good," said Striker, picking up a small glass for himself. He drained it quickly and, feeling a little cooler, headed back into the hunt. He left Ralph behind him, still exclaiming about the punch.

"Hey! I got one with money in it!" Striker heard a voice shout. He turned and saw Ralph's best friend, Jason Hill, waving a red egg in the air. "Awesome!"

Striker shrugged and went back to searching.

After about five minutes, Striker had collected six more eggs. He was working his way around the edge of the house. He was so intent on looking that he almost bumped into the punch table, where Ralph was once again guzzling punch. "Careful, Striker," shouted Ralph. "You don't want to spill any of this delicious punch."

Nearby, Jason Hill found another yellow egg. Striker watched him open it and saw that this one too, contained money. Once again, he shrugged and continued searching.

After a few more minutes, Striker again almost bumped into something—this time it was Bill.

"Sorry," laughed Striker. "How are you doing?"

"I'm doing all right. Not as many as I'd like."

"Bill," said Striker, "You've got to be kidding me. It looks like you've got about 35 eggs. I've only got 11."

"All the same, I'm going to need more to win. Plus, all my eggs have only had candy in them, but Jason Hill has found at least seven eggs with money inside! I've got to catch up. See you later." Bill waved at Striker and then dove back into the bushes.

Striker smiled at Bill's antics, and then caught sight of Jason searching for eggs. "Maybe he's just really lucky," thought Striker.

He had just started looking for eggs again by the Johnsons' grill when he overheard Ralph talking to his father.

"You know, Dad," Ralph was saying loudly, "I think this punch gets better with every sip I take."

"Thanks, Son," said Mr. Johnson, laughing, "but I think you're going a little overboard."

"No, I'm serious," said Ralph. "Every single cup is better than the one before it. It's just amazing. I could drink it all day."

Upon hearing this statement, Striker stopped searching for eggs. He stood still for a moment, apparently lost in thought. Finally, he snapped out of it and began to rummage around in his pocket. He pulled out two rubber bands and a toy car before he found what he was looking for: a small pencil. He quickly took a piece of candy out of one of his eggs, popped it into his mouth, and began writing a note on the wrapper. Once he finished, he folded the note and placed it back in the empty egg. Then, he walked over to Ralph, passing Jason on his way, who had again found an egg with money in it.

"Here, Ralph," said Striker, "I think you dropped this." He threw the egg into Ralph's free hand, ignoring his protests that he wasn't even playing. Striker walked away as Ralph cracked open the egg.

From inside the egg, Ralph pulled out Striker's wrapper. Upon reading the note, his face paled. He clenched his hands and glared after Striker.

While Ralph glowered at his retreating back, Striker joined Bill who was vigorously searching a flowerbed.

"Hey, Bill, check this out."

Bill turned to look where Striker was pointing.

"This better be important," said Bill, "if you're making me waste valuable egg-searching time."

"Just watch," replied Striker. "You'll enjoy it."

Ralph was carefully tearing the wrapper into tiny pieces, still shooting dirty looks at Striker. After a moment, however, Ralph slowly walked over to Jason. He whispered something to Jason, who began to look rather angry himself. The two boys argued for a moment and then reluctantly began to put Jason's eggs back into the bushes.

Suddenly Striker heard a soft voice behind him. "What's that all about?"

Striker turned to see Sheila looking over his shoulder.

He swallowed hard and tried to sound casual. "Oh, Ralph and Jason were cheating, that's all."

How did Striker know?

Solution

While it was pretty fishy that Ralph was spending so much time at the punch table, Striker really took notice when he heard Ralph say that every cup of punch was better than the one before it. Now, that's almost never true. Instead, the more you have of something, the less tasty it seems. For instance, the second Coke is never better than the first Coke, and the third Coke isn't even as good as the second. So, Striker knew that Ralph was making up how much he was enjoying the punch.

If Ralph wasn't really enjoying each cup of punch more than the previous cup, then he must have had some other reason for saying so. That part was easy when Striker thought about the facts—Ralph knew where the eggs were hidden, and his best friend Jason kept finding the ones with money. Striker realized they must have set up some sort of signal where Ralph would praise the punch every time Jason was near a money egg.

As Ralph and Jason replaced the eggs, Striker explained all this to Bill and Sheila. Bill laughed and said, "Even if I don't win today, it was worth it to see the look on Ralph's face!" He gave Striker a quick high-five and then hurried off to search for more eggs, straightening his bandana as he went. Striker noticed that he went straight to the areas where Ralph and Jason had just put back some eggs.

After Bill was gone, Striker was left alone with Sheila, and he could feel the butterflies begin.

Now, whenever Striker solved a mystery, he always tried very hard to be modest. This time, though, he couldn't help but feel a tiny bit proud when Sheila gave him one long, admiring look and his butterflies faded away.

Striker Jones, "The Egg Hunt Hoodwink"

Lesson Plan

Objective: Students will be able to explain and apply the economic law of diminishing marginal utility, though you may wish to avoid this technical terminology with younger students.

Procedure

1. Read the chapter "The Egg Hunt Hoodwink" up until the Solution, either as a class or separately.

2. In pairs or small groups, have students discuss what they believe is the solution to the mystery.

3. Read the Solution as a class.

4. As a class, define the words *diminishing* (decreasing), *marginal* (at the outer limits—in other words, what happens when we add just one more), and *utility* (the good that we get out of something, pleasure).

5. Check for understanding with the following questions:

    - What specific comment of Ralph's caught Striker's attention? ("Every single cup [of punch] is better than the one before it.")

    - Why did it catch his attention? (While Ralph could still be enjoying the punch, it wouldn't actually be getting better as he drank more and more. In fact, it would be less enjoyable the more he had.)

- Imagine that Bill has chocolate in each of the eggs he collected. If he sat down and ate all of the chocolate at once, would it taste better at the beginning or the end? Why? (The beginning. As he has more and more chocolate, the pleasure he gets from it will fade.)

6. Discuss the concept of diminishing marginal utility. Key points include the following:

    - Diminishing marginal utility is a fancy way of saying that the more you have of something, the less you enjoy it. This applies to all kinds of things: food and drink, fun activities, songs you like, even summer vacation!

    - You can really tell the law of diminishing marginal utility is in place when you overeat. Maybe that first piece of pizza is delicious. The second might be almost as good. The third is so-so. Now imagine that you kept going until you'd eaten 20 pieces of pizza! You'd feel so sick by then that you wouldn't be enjoying it at all!

7. Class Activity: Pass out a bag of 10 Starbursts to each student. Have each student draw a graph at their desk with *utility* (or *pleasure*, for younger students) on the vertical axis on a scale of 1-10 and *# of Starbursts* on the horizontal axis. Eat each Starburst one at a time, and have each student mark on their graph how they rate the satisfaction of each. Once all 10 are consumed and all points have been plotted, students should draw a line through all points to create a line graph. Have students compare with each other the shape of their graphs. Discuss as a class if you notice any overall trends.

Assignment

Come up with three activities where you've experienced diminishing marginal utility. That means that, as you did the activity more, it became less enjoyable and you became ready to try something else. This could happen over the course of a few years or just over an afternoon!

"The Egg Hunt Hoodwink" Lesson

Chapter 9

Museums and Mummies,

Dinos and Daisies

"I am so excited about this field trip. I've never seen dinosaur bones before!" said Bill.

It was a sunny Friday morning, and Striker's whole class was gathered on the bus ramp getting ready to embark on the annual end-of-year field trip. This year, they were going to the Natural History Museum.

"I mean, real dinosaurs!" continued Bill. "It doesn't get any cooler than that!"

"Except for maybe the mummies," said Striker. "I've heard those are awesome."

"Oooh, the mummies sound terrifying!" said Sheila. "Are they real?"

"I think so," said Striker. "But they'll be behind glass and stuff. I'm sure we're not allowed to touch them."

"Still. . ." Sheila shivered and smiled.

"What's the matter, Sheila?" someone sneered from behind Striker. "Scared of a few mummies?"

Striker turned with a groan to face Ralph and his best friend Jason.

"I should have known," he thought. Ralph had been giving all of them an especially hard time since the Easter egg hunt.

"Lay off, Ralph," said Striker.

"And who's going to make me, Striker? You're probably scared of the mummies, too," he laughed. "And who cares about dinosaurs? What are you, five years old?"

"Oh, come on, you don't think dinosaurs are cool?" said Bill. He crossed his arms. "You're lying."

"Am not. Jason and I don't care about that kid stuff anyways. We want to see the weapons exhibit."

"What weapons exhibit?" asked Amy.

"Everyone knows the Natural History Museum has a huge display of guns and knives," said Jason.

"We'll probably be too sissy to go visit it as a class, so Jason and I are going to sneak off to go see them for ourselves."

"Sounds great," said Striker, rolling his eyes.

"Yeah," added Bill. "We'll really miss you."

Amy and Sheila laughed.

"Think that's funny?" Ralph demanded.

"Excuse me, Ralph," said a sweet voice. Ralph shrunk back and turned to face their teacher, Ms. Peters.

"Yes, Ms. Peters?" he asked, trying, and failing, to sound innocent.

"You don't look very busy right now. Why don't you come help me carry some of these heavy coolers? You too, Jason. We've got a lot of lunches to load on the bus."

"Oh, ok," Ralph muttered. After a warning glance from the teacher, he meekly added, "I mean, yes, Ms. Peters." He and Jason walked in the direction of the bus with shoulders slumped.

"Carry on, kids," said Ms. Peters with a wink before she turned to follow Ralph and Jason.

"I hope they get lost at the museum," said Amy.

When the class first reached the museum, they all had to wait out front with a few volunteer parents while Ms. Peters went inside to gather their tickets. There was a wide lawn that stretched across the front of the enormous building, perfect for a group of kids killing time. Some of the students got up a game of tag, while others did cartwheels and spun in circles.

Daisies were growing in the grass, attracting the attention of a few of the girls. While the kids played, two students, Rosie Marivaux and Julia Linchfield, began to weave flower crowns. Ms. Peters took so long to get the tickets, that Rosie and Julia had time to make crowns for themselves and several extras for some of their friends.

Sheila and Amy watched them from the shade of a hickory tree. "Oooh, I want one," said Sheila. "Don't you?"

"Nah," said Amy. "Flowers aren't really my thing. But if you want one, why don't you go ask if you can have one of the extras they've made?"

"Because look at all the girls who want them." And indeed, there was quite a crowd of girls surrounding Julia and Rosie now, all wanting their own flower crowns. "I'd never get one," Sheila finished.

Just then, Ms. Peters emerged from the front of the museum. "All right, students," she called. "We're ready to go. Let's line up!"

Sheila sighed. "Well, no time to make my own now."

Everyone rushed to be first in line, and the flower crowns were all but forgotten.

The first exhibit the class saw was the gems and minerals room. Everyone was amazed at the different kinds of rocks they saw.

"I love the sparkly ones," said Amy. "Can you imagine finding one of these in your backyard?"

"Look!" shouted Bill across the room. "I found some lava!"

Striker hurried over to see for himself. "Why's it black?" he asked, looking at the coal-black rock filled with holes. "I thought lava was bright red."

"It is," said Bill, reading from the sign. "But this is how it looks once it's cooled."

"Awesome."

Nearby, Striker and Bill could overhear Rosie talking to Julia.

"These are so gorgeous," she was saying, looking at a display of sapphires. "I could spend all day in this room."

"I know," agreed Julia. "I wish we could."

They were quiet a moment, before Rosie continued.

"Did I tell you that Christina Martin offered me her chocolate chip cookies for a flower crown?"

"No, you didn't. Did you take it?"

"Nah. But I thought it was kind of neat. We could practically start our own business!"

Julia laughed.

Just then, Striker was bumped from behind, hard.

"Oh, excuse me," said Ralph with a sneer. "I didn't see you."

Striker narrowed his eyes, but then felt a hand on his arm.

"Just ignore him," said Sheila.

"I'm trying," said Striker. "But one of these days…"

"I know. Here, come look at this geode that Bill found. It's really cool."

The geode was a rock that looked very bumpy on the outside, but was filled with sparkly blue crystal formations on the inside.

"Kind of makes you want to break open every rock you see, doesn't it?" said Sheila. "You never know when that might be inside."

Striker and Bill agreed.

After the gems and minerals, the class moved on to the mummy exhibit that Striker was so looking forward to. It was everything he'd hoped it would be. The mummies and the other artifacts from Ancient Egypt were very fragile, so the lights had to be kept very low to protect them. With the partial darkness, the exhibit felt extra mysterious, and Striker felt a little shiver go down his spine when he first saw a mummy up close. He couldn't stop himself from looking around for Ralph and Jason. "Let's see if they're really as tough as they say," he thought. But he didn't see them in the dim room.

After spending twenty minutes looking at burial scrolls and sarcophaguses, and even a stone taken from an actual pyramid, they proceeded to what was the crowning exhibit of the day—the Hall of Dinosaurs. Bill was particularly excited as he stared at the huge skeleton of a Tyrannosaurus Rex.

"Wow," said Bill, staring straight up into the wide jaws of the dinosaur. "Can you believe it, Striker? A real T-Rex?"

"It's pretty awesome," said Striker "Can you imagine meeting that thing in the wild?"

"It'd be scary," said Bill. He cleared his throat. "To most people, that is. *I* wouldn't be scared."

"Of course not," said Striker, hiding a smile.

"You know," continued Bill after a moment, "whenever I see dinosaur bones on TV, I always wonder about what would happen if I accidentally knocked into a skeleton. Couldn't you just see the bones flying everywhere?"

Striker certainly could. In his mind's eye, he watched the dinosaur skeleton come crashing to the ground, bones ricocheting off the floor and the walls. The dinosaur's head alone could probably crush the heavy wooden table next to them.

Striker was quiet for a moment, enjoying the thought.

"We'd probably get in trouble," said Bill.

"Yeah. Big trouble," agreed Striker.

The boys stared up at the bones in silence.

"Too bad," they both sighed together.

"Excuse me, class. I need everyone's attention."

The boys turned to the head of the Hall of Dinosaurs where Ms. Peters was addressing the class. She looked worried.

"We're missing a couple students, and I need to know if anyone knows where they might have gone."

Striker and Bill looked at each other.

"Does anyone know the location of Ralph and Jason?"

Bill raised his hand. "Ms. Peters, they said that they wanted to go see the weapons exhibit while we were here."

"Thank you, Bill, but I'm afraid we've already checked the other exhibits in the museum. They aren't there."

The class began murmuring in excitement. Ms. Peters turned to confer with the volunteer parents.

Striker thought back to the conversation he had overhead in the gem room between Rosie and Julia. Ralph must have been right behind him at the time, because he knocked into Striker only seconds later.

Striker raised his hand. "Ms. Peters," he said loudly over the noise, "I think I know where Ralph and Jason are."

The room went quiet.

"Where is that, Striker?"

"They're probably on the front lawn."

Why?

Solution

      Whenever a lot of people really want something, then enterprising businesses will usually respond by making a whole lot of that something to meet the increased demand. For instance, if lots of people want cupcakes, then bakers respond by making lots of cupcakes to sell. Plus, not only do bakers make more cupcakes, it also attracts more people to become bakers. Then, you have even more cupcakes!

      The same principle works for flower crowns. Striker knew lots of people wanted the flower crowns that Julia and Rosie were making. After all, they had quickly run out of all the crowns they'd made, and students were even offering to exchange parts of their lunches for a crown! He also knew that Ralph had overhead that the crowns were in high demand, and he could just imagine Ralph and Jason salivating over what they could get in exchange for more crowns.

      The only place to make more crowns was the lawn in front of the museum. So, when Ralph and Jason went missing, it seemed like a likely spot to find them.

Striker was right. When Ms. Peters found Ralph and Jason sitting in the field making flower crowns, she was furious. The whole class looked on laughing through a museum window as the teacher gave the two boys a very stern lecture. Even funnier than the lecture was the sight of Ralph and Jason surrounded by flowers and some of the ugliest, most ill-shaped flower crowns they'd ever seen.

"Don't quit your day job, Ralph," thought Striker with a chuckle.

Ms. Peters marched the boys back into the museum where they had to spend the remainder of the day sitting on a bench in the front hallway.

At the end of the day, the class headed back to the buses. As they walked back across the lawn, Striker noticed something lying in the daisy field. There was one single daisy crown left behind from where Julia and Rosie had been working. He slipped it into his jacket pocket and tried to work up the courage to give it to a certain someone on the way home.

Striker Jones, "Museums and Mummies, Dinos and Daisies"

Lesson Plan

Objective: Students will be able to explain and apply the economic concepts of supply and demand and competition.

Procedure

1. Read the chapter "Museums and Mummies, Dinos and Daisies" up until the Solution, either as a class or separately.

2. In pairs or small groups, have students discuss what they believe is the solution to the mystery.

3. Read the Solution as a class.

4. As a class, define the words *supply* (the amount of a good that is available for purchase), *demand* (the desire and ability to purchase something), and competition (a rivalry between people, groups, or firms).

5. Check for understanding with the following questions:

    - In the story, there was a lot of demand for the flower crowns. That is, lots of kids wanted one. How do we know that? (Julia and Rosie were surrounded by a big crowd wanting one. People were willing to trade for them. They eventually ran out of crowns, and people (like Sheila) still wanted more!)

    - Julia and Rosie weren't able to supply as many crowns as they would have liked. Why? (They had to make the crowns in the garden in front of the museum, but they didn't get to spend too much time there.)

- Why do Ralph and Jason go back to the garden, even when they weren't supposed to? (To make crowns so that they could charge for them; to provide competition to Julia and Rosie and increase the supply of flower crowns.)

6. Discuss the concepts of supply and demand and competition. Key points include the following:

    - Supply is how much of something is produced. Demand is the flip side—how many people want to buy what is being produced. Supply and demand are constantly changing and interact with each other all the time.

    - You see the results of supply and demand every time you go to the store. Suppliers produce the product and demanders buy it. If you didn't have suppliers, there would be no product to buy. If you had no demanders, no one would buy the product, and suppliers would stop making it!

    - Ralph and Jason go back to make more flower crowns in response to all the demand. This also happens in the real world. When goods are very popular, new people are attracted into the field and start making those products, too. After all, people are just waiting to buy the goods!

    - When new suppliers enter the field, like Ralph and Jason did, that is competition. Buyers are made better off by competition, because suppliers compete for their business by trying to make better and better products. If only Ralph and Jason hadn't been so bad at making flower crowns, the other students could have taken advantage of the competition!

7. Class Activity: Have students work in pairs to come up with an idea for a business that they could start. They should be providing either a good or service. Have them discuss how they would go about supplying that good or service with their own special talents. Then have them consider demand: who might want to buy their product and why?

Assignment

At home, pick out your favorite drink (or type of food, toy, piece of clothing, etc.). Have a parent help you find the contact information of the company that produces that drink. (You can sometimes find this information on the label, or you could look online.) Then, write a thank you note to a representative of the company for producing a good which you are able to enjoy. Tell the company why you like the drink and why your family buys it!

"Museums and Mummies, Dinos and Daisies" Lesson

Chapter 10

The Surprise Story

"Dad!" called Striker on the first Saturday morning of summer vacation. "Are you busy?"

"Not particularly," his dad called back from his study. "Why?"

"I need something to do," yelled Striker.

"Why don't you call one of your friends?" called his dad.

"But I still wouldn't know what to do with them," shouted Striker.

"You could play outside."

"It's too hot."

"Then you could play inside," Mr. Jones shouted.

"I don't suppose," interrupted Mrs. Jones walking into the hall, "that we could try doing something without having to scream back and forth about it?"

"Sorry," yelled Striker.

"Sorry," yelled his dad.

His mom sighed.

Striker wandered into the kitchen, and hopped onto a barstool. He draped himself across the counter.

His mom laughed as she wiped the countertop around him. "What is it?"

"I'm bored, Mom. What should I do?"

"Well," said Mrs. Jones, "didn't I hear you say earlier that you got some early birthday money from your grandparents?"

"Yeah," said Striker.

"Why don't you go do something fun with it?"

"But I can't think of anything!"

"Honestly, Striker," said Mrs. Jones, "I have never known you to be so unimaginative."

"Well," said Striker's dad, who had just walked in the door, "I can think of plenty of things to keep you busy." He started ticking off on his fingers. "The car needs to be washed; the gutters are dirty; your bathroom is a mess."

"Ok, ok," said Striker hurriedly, sitting up. "Maybe I can think of something to do."

"I thought I could help you see the light," said Mr. Jones.

"Hey," said Striker, "you know what could be cool?"

"What's that?" asked him mom.

"The arcade's got a new game in called Dance Pants. It's one of those games where you have to make the right movements along with the music. And Bill is really, really good at it, but I think I could take him if I practiced." Striker was getting excited. "Plus, I could use my early birthday money to pay for it!"

"Sounds like a good idea," said Mr. Jones.

"Yeah! I'll do that!" Striker jumped up. "I'm going to call Bill and ask if he wants to go, too. Can you take us, Dad?"

Mr. Jones checked his watch. "I can take you, but not yet. I've got a meeting in an hour on that side of town. Gas is getting pretty expensive, so I'd like to combine the trips. Just tell Bill we'll pick him up then, and I'll come back and get you guys up from the arcade after the meeting."

"Ok, Dad. Thanks!" Striker went to call Bill.

"This game is so totally awesome!" shouted Striker as he and Bill struggled to hit all the right moves at the right time.

"I know!" said Bill, crisscrossing his legs back and forth.

"How did you do that?" shouted Striker. He tried crossing his legs the same way Bill had, but only succeeded in tripping and falling off the side of the dance mat.

"Whoa," he yelled as he hit the floor. He jumped up again immediately, rubbing his backside as he did so.

"Good luck catching up now," laughed Bill.

"Watch it, or I'll 'accidentally' trip in your direction!" said Striker, jumping back into the game.

Bill's feet were flashing back and forth so quickly that he was attracting a crowd of other kids. They gathered around the game and quickly took up the chant, "Go Bill! Go Bill! Go Bill!" Striker got a few cheers as well, but Bill was obviously the star of this game. Every now and then, even Striker would catch himself being distracted by Bill's fancy footwork. Then he'd have to shake his head clear and try and catch up again, more behind than ever. He wiped the sweat off his forehead, and concentrated on not tripping in front of the crowd. All told, he was having a great time.

After another half hour of Dance Pants, Striker was completely worn out. He and Bill had finished the game to a wild outburst of applause from the crowd, and then promptly collapsed on the floor in the corner of the arcade.

"Man," said Bill, still out of breath. "That was awesome."

"No kidding," said Striker. "I can't believe how good you are."

"Aw, it's nothing," Bill said. He rolled onto his back and stretched his legs out, first his right, then his left. "Geez, I am going to be so sore tomorrow!"

"Yeah, me too," muttered Striker tiredly from the floor.

"I'm sure you will," said a voice from behind Striker's head. He tipped his head backward on the floor so that he could see the person standing just behind him. When he saw who it was, he quickly jumped up from the floor.

"Oh, hi, Sheila," he said, suddenly sounding much more energized. "I didn't realize you were here."

"Sure," said Sheila. "Amy and I have been watching almost since you guys started."

"Oh really?" asked Striker. Inside his thoughts were dwelling unpleasantly on his fall off the mat. "Did she see?" he wondered.

"Nice fall," said another voice behind Striker. He turned to see Amy.

"I guess they saw," he thought with a groan.

Bill laughed. "Yeah, that was pretty spectacular, Striker."

Sheila turned to Striker. "Are you going to play any more today?"

Striker thought of his aching feet and legs. He was worn out. "I don't think so," he said. "Not that I'm tired or anything," he added quickly. "I just need to get home." He thought a moment. "You know, though, I do have lots of quarters left. Does anyone want to come back with me tomorrow?"

"Sorry, man," said Bill. "My dad's already told me I'll be doing yard work all day. I don't think I can get out of it."

"Bummer," said Striker. "What about you two?" he asked, turning to Sheila and Amy.

"Can't," said Amy. "We're going out of town to visit my grandma."

"I'm sorry, Striker, but I can't either," said Sheila. "My sister's got a dance recital that I have to go to."

"Oh, ok," said Striker, trying not to show his disappointment.

"Maybe we can come with you next weekend for your birthday," said Bill.

"That'd be cool," said Striker. "Anyways, my legs probably won't be working by tomorrow anyhow. Speaking of which…" He fished a coin out of his pocket. "I don't suppose anybody would be willing to carry me to the car for a quarter, huh?"

"I thought you weren't tired," teased Amy.

"I'm not," said Striker quickly. "Just a joke, Amy, just a joke." And with that, he started walking toward the door to the parking lot, doing his best not to limp.

The next day, Striker resolved to go to the arcade by himself. He knew it wouldn't be quite as much fun without his friends there, but he still really wanted to practice. He wandered into his dad's study to ask for a ride.

"Hey, Dad," he began, "are you headed into town any time soon?"

"Well, not right away," said Mr. Jones, "But I do have a committee meeting at church later this afternoon. Why?"

"Oh, I was just hoping you might take me to the arcade." Striker turned to leave.

"Sure. I can take you right now, as a matter of fact," said his dad.

"Really?" asked Striker, stopping in the doorway. "Don't you want to combine trips to save on gas?"

"Oh, that's ok. I don't want you to have to wait just to save a little money." He stood up from his desk. "Are you ready to go?"

An hour and a half later, Striker sat waiting outside the arcade for his dad to pick him up. His time playing Dance Pants hadn't been nearly as fun as before. Without Bill there, Striker couldn't reach some of the higher levels, so he had spent most of his time on lower levels that were a little boring. Then, to make matters worse, a kid about three years younger than him had started to play the game as well and was much better than Striker. After being repeatedly outshone, Striker decided he'd had enough of the arcade and called his dad to pick him up.

Now he sat on the curb waiting, idly twirling a blade of grass between his fingers. It was very hot outside. Striker could even see waves of heat rising off the pavement of the gas station next door. As he looked at the heat waves, another sight caught his eye—the sign showing the prices of gasoline. From the looks of it, the price of gas had risen over the past day.

"Hmm," thought Striker. "Gas has gone up. But Dad didn't mind making a special trip for me this morning, in spite of the prices. Weird."

Just then, his dad pulled into the parking lot. As Striker walked to the car, he wondered about his dad's actions.

"Hey, Dad," he said, getting into the car.

"Hi, Striker," said Mr. Jones. "How was the arcade?"

"Oh, it was ok," said Striker. On the ride home, he tried to keep up a conversation with his dad, but he kept being distracted by his own thoughts.

"Yesterday," Striker thought, "Dad made me wait to go to the arcade so that he could combine trips. That saved money on gasoline… So far," he thought to himself, "everything makes sense."

He scratched his head. "But today, with gas even more expensive than before, Dad didn't make me wait till he was on his way to town. The costs had gone up, but he didn't seem to care. Why?"

The car had pulled up in front of their house. As Striker got out, he gave his dad a suspicious look. Had his dad been trying to get rid of him this morning?

Striker walked up the front sidewalk and onto the front porch. He paused for a moment with his hand on the doorknob to give his father one more curious look. His dad only smiled.

Striker pushed open the door slowly while he wondered, "But why would Dad want to get me out of the house?"

"SURPRISE!" The roar of sound swept over Striker as he looked confusedly into his living room. As he focused on the room, he froze in the doorway in shock. Suddenly, in a rush, all the clues fell into place. Of course! He was having a surprise party!

Slowly, Striker's look of disbelief changed into a grin that spread from ear to ear. His living room was absolutely packed with people. First, he saw his mom standing and smiling by a large chocolate cake. Then, he saw Jim, wearing contacts, of course, and his best friend Zack. Rosie and Julia were sitting together by the fireplace, each wearing a flower crown. His music teacher was there with her new husband Mr. Larson, and he noticed his homeroom teacher Ms. Peters sipping a Dr. Pepper by the snack table. Even Ralph and his friend Jason were slouching in a corner, throwing the occasional dirty look at the other guests.

But best of all, Striker saw his three best friends, Bill, Sheila, and Amy, standing in front of the entire crowd. Amy and Sheila were wearing party hats, while Bill was happily blowing a noisemaker.

His dad clapped him on the back from behind. "We really got you, didn't we?"

Striker nodded, still too surprised to speak.

His mother came forward holding the birthday cake, and Striker saw that she was smiling as brightly as the lit birthday candles. Mr. Jones flipped off the lights for dramatic effect, and the whole room broke into a chorus of "Happy Birthday."

At the end of the song, Striker paused to make his birthday wish, but looking at his friends and family around him, he found he didn't have much else to wish for.

So instead, he just smiled and blew out the candles.

After every last candle had been extinguished, his dad called out, "Now, let's cut that cake! We've got two celebrations on our hands!"

"What do you mean, *two* celebrations?" asked Striker.

"Well, of course, first, there's your birthday," said Mr. Jones. "And second," he paused with a twinkle in his eye, "something very extraordinary happened today!"

"Really?" asked Striker curiously. "What?"

Mr. Jones smiled and put an arm around his son. "Let's just put it this way—," he said with a laugh. "It's not everyday we manage to pull a fast one on Striker Jones."

Striker Jones, "The Surprise Story"

Lesson Plan

Objective: Students will be able to explain and apply the economic concepts of prices and price sensitivity.

Procedure

1. Read the chapter "The Surprise Story."

2. As a class, define the words *price* (how much money is charged for a good or service) and *sensitivity* (how easily you are affected by something).

3. Check for understanding with the following questions:

    - In the beginning of the story, Striker's dad arranges his behavior according to the price of gas. Can you give the example? (He says that gas is expensive, so he'd like to combine the trip to his meeting with taking Striker to the arcade).

    - How would you expect Striker's dad to react when the price of gas goes even higher at the end of the story? (Striker's dad would want to use less gas. So, he might drive even less. He might combine more trips. He might walk more places. Etc.)

    - Instead, what happens? (Striker's dad doesn't mind making a special trip to take Striker to the arcade.)

- Why did Striker's dad do this? (To get Striker out of the house for a surprise party!)

4. Discuss the concept of prices and price sensitivity. Key points include the following:

    - All goods and services have some sort of price if you want to buy them. When we talk about prices, we're usually talking about a dollar amount, although really, it could be anything that it costs you to get a good or service.

    - Prices are very important because they help us direct our resources in the best way possible. Prices give us an idea of how much something is worth. So, if we only have a set amount of money, we can make decisions about how to divide it up among the huge variety of goods and services that are available!

    - Prices are set as a combination of the number of people who want an item (demand) and the amount of the item that is available to buy (supply). They move up and down as supply and demand for a product change. For instance, if lots of people want something (high demand), the price goes up.

    - Prices can affect our behavior, like in the story with Striker's dad. How much a change in price affects our behavior is called price sensitivity. That describes how much we'd change in response to a price change.

5. Class Activity: Have each student pick one item from their desk to put up "for sale." Have them mark the price for their item with a note card or sticky note. Once all prices are

marked, encourage students to walk around the room to see what's available. Then, tally the various items and their prices on the blackboard. Use these tallies to lead a discussion about how prices affect buying habits. For instance, if five rulers are available for different prices, which would they buy and why? When would they be willing to pay more than the lowest price? If there's only one of a certain item for sale, how does that affect their decisions about price? Etc.

Assignment

We're all sensitive to prices in our daily lives. Sit down with your family and discuss what changes you would make in your behavior if the following happened:

- If electricity became more expensive.

- If the price of dining out went down.

- If gas became less expensive.

- If the cable bill went up.

- If clothing became more expensive.

- If going to the movies became free.

"The Surprise Story" Lesson

ABOUT THE AUTHOR

Maggie M. Larche is a Florida native currently enjoying Milwaukee, Wisconsin, where she resides with her husband and son. After receiving a master's in social sciences from the University of Chicago, she committed herself to bringing economic basics to today's youth. Striker Jones was born from her personal fondness for a good mystery.

Glossary of Possible Vocabulary Words

Includes both challenging words from the chapter and economic terms from the lesson.

Chapter 1 – "Shark Showdown"

Barter (v) - To trade.
Benefit (n) – A consequence that is good.
Commemorate (v) – To honor or memorialize an event or person.
Propose (v) – To offer or suggest.
Scarcity (n) – Having limited amounts of something.
Trek (n) – A difficult journey.
Wheeze (v) – To breathe with difficulty.

Chapter 2 – "The Missing Key"

Confiscate (v) – To seize from an authority position.
Cringe (v) – To wince in embarrassment or distaste.
Dutifully (adv) – Performing the duties expected of one.
Incentive (n) – A factor that motivates behavior.
Loss (n) – Costs minus revenue, losing money, the opposite of profit.
Profit (n) – Revenue minus costs, money coming in less money going out.
Shuffle (v) – To walk without lifting the feet.

Chapter 3 – "Risky Decisions"

Lure (v) – To attract or entice.
Pandemonium (n) – Wild and noisy uproar, chaos.
Risk (n) – The possibility of losing something or of incurring a loss.
Urge (v) – To attempt to persuade.

Chapter 4 – "Looks Like Love"

Amble (v) – To go at a slow, easy pace.
Good (n) – Products that can be seen and touched.
Grimace (v) – To make a facial expression that shows pain.
Opportunity Cost (n) – The next best thing that one gives up when one chooses one thing over another.
Service (n) – Work performed for others.

Chapter 5 – "Election Day"

Campaign (n) – The competition by rival candidates for office.
Coordinate (v) – To arrange and combine in appropriate order.
Influence (v) – To move or impel someone to action.
Nominate (v) – To propose or put forward one for elected office.
Represent (v) – To act for or on behalf of others.

Chapter 6 – "Smarts and Crafts"

Antsy (adj) – Restless or fidgety.
Exasperated (adj) - Extremely annoyed.
Grandiose (adj) – Very complicated or grand.
Private property (n) – Something that can be owned by someone.
Right (n) – Something to which one is entitled.
Strewn (adj) – Scattered or sprinkled about.
Unbeknownst (adj) – Unknown.

Chapter 7 – "Auction Action"

Asymmetry (n) – Unequal, one side having more than another.
Auction (n) – A sale at which things are sold to the highest bidder.
Bid (v) – To offer the price one is willing pay.
Categorize (v) – To classify.
Conspicuous (adj) – Easily noticed.
Information (n) – Knowledge that one possesses.
Murmur (v) – A low, continuous sound of indistinct voices.
Speculate (v) – To think, wonder, or reflect.

Chapter 8 – "The Egg Hunt Hoodwink"

Antic (n) – A playful trick.
Diminishing (adj) – Decreasing or going down.
Hoodwink (v) – To deceive or trick.
Marginal (adj) – At the outer limits.
Utility (n) – The good or pleasure that one gets out of something.

Chapter 9 – "Museums and Mummies, Dinos and Daisies"

Competition (n) – A rivalry between people, groups, or firms.
Confer (v) – To consult together.
Demand (n) – The desire and ability to purchase a good or service.
Embark (v) – To start an enterprise, journey, or task.
Geode (n) – A hollow stone often lined with crystals.
Meekly (adv) – Humbly patient or compliant.
Ricochet (v) – To bounce one or more times off of a surface.
Sarcophagus (n) – A stone coffin.
Supply (n) – The amount of a good or service that is available for purchase.

Chapter 10 – "The Surprise Story"

Committee (n) – A group elected or appointed to perform some function.
Dramatic (adj) – Theatrical.
Extraordinary (adj) – Beyond what is usual, special.
Idle (adj) – Not working or active.
Price (n) – How much money is charged for a good or service.
Sensitivity (n) – How easily one is affected by something.

Common Core State Standards in English and Language Arts Addressed by *Striker Jones*

Each chapter is listed with the economic concepts covered and lesson alignments with 1) the English Language Arts Common Core State Standards and 2) the voluntary national economic standards set by the National Council on Economic Education (NCEE).

Chapter 1: Shark Showdown
Economic Concepts: Bartering, Scarcity, Value, Mutual Benefits of Trade
Aligned to English Language Arts Common Core Standards:
    L.3.6, L.4.6, L.5.6
    RL.3.1, RL.4.1, RL.5.1, RL.3.3, RL.4.3
    RI.3.1, RI.4.1, RI.5.1, RI.3.3, RI.4.3, RI.3.4, RI.4.4, RI.5.4
Aligned to NCEE Standards: 1, 5, 7, 8

Chapter 2: The Missing Key
Economic Concepts: Profits, Loss, Incentives, Arbitrage, Morality in Markets
Aligned to English Language Arts Common Core Standards:
    L.3.6, L.4.6, L.5.6
    RL.3.1, RL.4.1, RL.5.1, RL.3.3, RL.4.3
    RI.3.1, RI.4.1, RI.5.1, RI.3.3, RI.4.3, RI.3.4, RI.4.4, RI.5.4
Aligned to NCEE Standards: 5, 14

Chapter 3: Risky Decisions
Economic Concepts: Risks, Benefits
Aligned to English Language Arts Common Core Standards:
    L.3.6, L.4.6, L.5.6
    RL.3.1, RL.4.1, RL.5.1, RL.3.3, RL.4.3
    RI.3.1, RI.4.1, RI.5.1, RI.3.3, RI.4.3, RI.3.4, RI.4.4, RI.5.4
Aligned to NCEE Standard: 4

Chapter 4: Looks Like Love
Economic Concepts: Goods vs. Services, Opportunity Cost, Businesses
Aligned to English Language Arts Common Core Standards:
    L.3.6, L.4.6, L.5.6
    RL.3.1, RL.4.1, RL.5.1, RL.5.3
    RI.3.1, RI.4.1, RI.5.1, RI.3.3, RI.4.3, RI.3.4, RI.4.4, RI.5.4
Aligned to NCEE Standards: 4, 13, 14

Chapter 5: Election Day
Economic Concepts: Voting, Public Choice
Aligned to English Language Arts Common Core Standards:
    L.3.6, L.4.6, L.5.6
    RL.3.1, RL.4.1, RL.5.1, RL.3.3, RL.4.3, RL.5.3
    RI.3.1, RI.4.1, RI.5.1, RI.3.3, RI.4.3, RI.3.4, RI.4.4, RI.5.4, RI.4.8, RI.5.8
Aligned to NCEE Standards: 4, 17

Chapter 6: Smarts and Crafts
Economic Concepts: Incentives, Private Property Rights
Aligned to English Language Arts Common Core Standards:
    L.3.6, L.4.6, L.5.6
    RL.3.1, RL.4.1, RL.5.1, RL.3.3
    RI.3.1, RI.4.1, RI.5.1, RI.3.3, RI.4.3, RI.3.4, RI.4.4, RI.5.4
Aligned to NCEE Standards: 4, 10

Chapter 7: Auction Action
Economic Concepts: Information Asymmetry, Value
Aligned to English Language Arts Common Core Standards:
    L.3.6, L.4.6, L.5.6
    RL.3.1, RL.4.1, RL.5.1, RL.3.3
    RI.3.1, RI.4.1, RI.5.1, RI.3.3, RI.4.3, RI.3.4, RI.4.4, RI.5.4
Aligned to NCEE Standards: 4, 7, 8

Chapter 8: The Egg Hunt Hoodwink
Economic Concepts: Diminishing Marginal Utility
Aligned to English Language Arts Common Core Standards:
    L.3.6, L.4.6, L.5.6
    RL.3.1, RL.4.1, RL.5.1
    RI.3.1, RI.4.1, RI.5.1, RI.3.3, RI.4.3, RI.3.4, RI.4.4, RI.5.4, RI.4.8, RI.5.8
Aligned to NCEE Standards: 2, 4

Chapter 9: Museums and Mummies, Dinos and Daisies
Economic Concepts: Supply, Demand, Competition
Aligned to English Language Arts Common Core Standards:
    L.3.6, L.4.6, L.5.6
    RL.3.1, RL.4.1, RL.5.1, RL.3.3, RL.5.3
    RI.3.1, RI.4.1, RI.5.1, RI.3.3, RI.4.3, RI.3.4, RI.4.4, RI.5.4, RI.4.8, RI.5.8
Aligned to NCEE Standards: 5, 6, 8, 9

Chapter 10: Surprise Story
Economic Concepts: Prices, Price Sensitivity
Aligned to English Language Arts Common Core Standards:
    L.3.6, L.4.6, L.5.6
    RL.3.1, RL.4.1, RL.5.1, RL.3.3, RL.4.3, RL.5.3
    RI.3.1, RI.4.1, RI.5.1, RI.3.3, RI.4.3, RI.3.4, RI.4.4, RI.5.4
Aligned to NCEE Standards: 4, 8

Made in the USA
Lexington, KY
15 May 2014